Aspects of modern sociolo

CW00871010

Social research

GENERAL EDITORS

John Barron Mays
Eleanor Rathbone Professor of Sociology, University of Liverpool

Maurice Craft
Senior Lecturer in Education, University of Exeter

BY THE SAME AUTHOR

School of Tomorrow (joint author) *(1968)*
Migration and Social Adjustment (joint author) *(1973)*

Sources of Official Data

Kathleen G. Pickett, B.Sc.

Senior Lecturer in Sociology
University of Liverpool

Longman

Longman
1724-1974

LONGMAN GROUP LIMITED
London and
Longman Inc., New York

Associated companies, branches and representatives throughout the world

© Longman Group Limited 1974

All rights reserved. No part of this publication may be reproduced, stored in a retrieval system, or transmitted in any form or by any means, electronic, mechanical, photocopying, recording, or otherwise, without the prior permission of the Copyright owner.

First published 1974

ISBN 0 582 48767.6 cased
        48768.4 paper
Library of Congress Catalog Card Number 73–86129

*Set by Libra Press Limited
and printed in Hong Kong
by Dai Nippon Printing Co. (HK) Ltd.*

Contents

Editors' Preface

The first series in Longman's *Aspects of modern sociology* library was concerned with the social structure of modern Britain, and was intended for students following professional and other courses in universities, polytechnics, colleges of education, and elsewhere in further and higher education, as well as for those members of a wider public wishing to pursue an interest in the nature and structure of British society.

This further series sets out to examine the history, aims, techniques and limitations of social research, and it is hoped that it will be of interest to the same readership. It will seek to offer an informative but not uncritical introduction to some of the methodologies of social science.

JOHN BARRON MAYS
MAURICE CRAFT

Acknowledgements

I would like to thank Mr D. Ramprakash, Statistician in the Office of Population Censuses and Surveys, for his help and advice concerning chapters 1 and 2, and members of the Department of Employment, North West Regional Office, Manchester, for similar aid with chapter 3. Errors and omissions remaining are entirely my responsibility, but without their help there would have been many more.

My thanks are also due to Mr Alan Neale, Statistician to Birmingham Corporation, for permission to reproduce his graph from the City of Birmingham Annual Abstract of Statistics (Figure 1).

I am also grateful to the following for permission to reproduce copyright material: The Controller of Her Majesty's Stationery Office for extracts from the *Registrar General's Statistical Review, Vols. I and II* and for the use of census and other official material and Liverpool University Press for extracts by H. Silcock from *Town Planning Review, Vol. XXIII, No. 4,* dated January 1953.

Foreword

The aim of this book is to provide a guide to some principal sources of statistical data which are published on a regular basis. In the first four chapters primary sources concerning population and other census topics, the labour force and education are examined. The information required in a research project investigating a group of individuals, geographically or functionally defined, has been the consideration—and material is presented with the sociologist, planner or other social investigator in mind. These subjects have been chosen principally because they are the topics with which such people are most often concerned; in addition, the last two—labour force and education—appear in an unusually wide variety of sources, often in different forms which may need to be reconciled. The census is basic to so much empirical research that it could not be omitted in any book on sources.

The book has also been written in the belief that there are a number of people involved in research, whether in universities, local government or some other organisation, who start with little or no knowledge of what information is available in published form, where it may be found, or how reliable it is when discovered. It is hoped that reference to these chapters will provide guidance for such people. Throughout, emphasis has been given to the method by which data have been collected, as this must clearly be the principal guide to their reliability and a key to their comparability.

The amount of published information available is continually increasing, and while this makes for difficulty in keeping up with the flow of material, it does mean that many serious gaps of early postwar years are now filled. Those responsible for this information are today more aware of such difficulties and have provided many new secondary sources in which material from a number of publications is brought together. While it is primary sources with which this guide is largely concerned, a list of secondary sources is given in the References section.

The final chapter on sampling frames has been added because it seems likely that the researcher whose work involves the organisation of a social survey is more often than not the one who will make substantial use of published data to provide a basis for his investigation, and may find guidance equally useful on available frames as available information.

Population and the Census 1

There are two principal sources of population data: the Census of Population and the Registrar General's Annual Estimates: the first is a primary source, the second derived. To these may be added a third, which, though not intended for such a purpose, can be used to provide supplementary information: the Electoral Register.

THE CENSUS OF POPULATION

This is the primary source of all population estimates. The administrative arrangements are nowadays made separately by the three Registrar Generals of England and Wales, Scotland, and Northern Ireland who are responsible for providing counts and estimates of the general population in their respective countries. For historical reasons, the Isle of Man and the Channel Islands both also conduct independent censuses but since 1951 the Census of Population has usually been taken simultaneously in all five areas, and in all but a few details, in identical form. An exception to this rule is the 1966 Census of Northern Ireland which was taken six months later than the other four, was a full Census and included fewer questions.

In a full Census of Population an attempt is made to count all those people in Great Britain and on British ships docked in her ports or in home waters on Census night. This has taken place every ten years since 1801, except in the wartime year 1941. Although provision for a five-year census was made in the Census Act of 1920, it was 1966 before the interval between Censuses was reduced, and then enumeration was on a 10 per cent sample basis (except in the Special Study Areas in Scotland where a complete enumeration was conducted: these areas are the counties of Roxburgh, Sutherland, Zetland; the towns of Fort William and Livingstone and their surrounding areas; and the islands of Lewis and Harris).

Since 1951 the Census has been taken on a Sunday night in mid-April—a time of year when relatively few people are away from home on holiday, but when weather conditions should be good enough to cause no great difficulty to the enumerator travelling round his area—the *Enumeration District*. However, on any day of the year there is always a proportion of people away from home—visiting, on business, in hospital and so on. The Census population as enumerated contains this element of abnormality, for—at least theoretically—each person is counted in the place at which they spend Census night.

At the upper level, the three Censuses of England and Wales, Scotland and Northern Ireland are combined to provide an enumerated population of Great Britain, while from the complete (100 per cent) Censuses, enumerated populations at every level down to wards within local authority areas are published, since 1961, including New Towns.

THE REGISTRAR GENERAL'S ANNUAL ESTIMATES

These estimates, also the responsibility of the Registrar Generals, are derived from the Census of Population.

Current estimates

The period between Censuses, even if reduced to five years, is too long to be without information on population size, a factor basic to so many central and local government decisions, to the size of local authority grants and countless other interests. Changes can occur rapidly and both increase and decrease on a large scale bring immediate needs. Since 1949, estimates of population valid for mid-year, 30 June, have been provided for inter-Census years (and for census year itself until a corrected version can be issued) for all standard areas down to local authority area level.

Projected estimates

A further responsibility of the Registrar General jointly with the Government Actuary is to provide estimates of future population. These have been published for England and Wales and Scotland since 1949, first in the December *Quarterly Returns* and since 1953 in the *Annual Statistical Review*, Part II (the *Civil* volume until 1957, and afterwards the *Population* volume). Until 1962, these projections were given for 5, 10, 15, 20, 30 and 40 years from the base year of the projection. Since then additional projections have been published for the earlier periods, and since 1964, the longer term projections are published for the same years—currently 1981, 1991 and 2001. These projections are revised as new trends appear to require the revision.

THE ELECTORAL REGISTER

The Electoral Register must be included as a source in spite of its limitations, for it can provide an annual count of population down to street level, if required, though only of those eligible to vote by the February following its publication. Since 1970 it has therefore included those aged eighteen years or more on that date; before 1970, those aged twenty-one years or more. A detailed description of the Register is given in chapter 5.

The publications in which population counts and estimates first appear, and the areas for which they are provided are given in Table 1.

PROBLEMS OF INTERPRETATION
Population definitions

Population estimates are provided in the following forms:

(a) Census enumerated population. Every person in Great Britain

3

TABLE I

Registrar General's population data for England and Wales : publications, area covered and associated variables

Publication		Population defined	Approximate date of publication	Area covered (see key)	Currently in association with :
CENSUS OF POPULATION					
Preliminary reports	1951	Provisional enumerated population (from enumerators' totals)	May 1951	⎱ 1–6	Sex
	1961		July 1961		Sex
	1971		August 1971		Sex
Advance analysis 1971		Provisional enumerated population extracted from schedule	December 1971–May 1972	1–5 + part 6*	Age, sex, marital status, economic activity and country of birth
1% sample	1951	Enumerated population sampled	July, Nov. 1952	⎱ 1–6	All census topics ⎱ see Table 2
	1971		August 1973		Some census topics
10% sample	1966	Enumerated sample population	1967	1–8	All census topics
		Enumerated sample population at usual residence	1969	1–6	Sex
Full Census	1951	Enumerated population	1953–55	1–6	All census topics ⎱ see Table 2
	1961		1963–64	1–8	All census topics
	1971		1972–730	1–9	All census topics
Full Census	1951	Enumerated population at usual residence	1956	1–6	Sex
	1961		1964	1–6	Sex
	1971		1974θ	1–6	Sex
ANNUAL STATISTICAL REVIEW					
Part I—Medical		Home population at 30 June year of issue	16–21 months after year of issue	1–6	
Part II—Population		Total population at 30 June year of issue	18–24 months after year of issue	1–6	Sex and age (Part 1), sex, age and marital status (Part II)
		Civilian population at 30 June year of issue		1	Sex and age

TABLE I (cont'd)

ANNUAL ESTIMATES	Provisional home population at current year, 30 June	December of current year	I-4, 6	—
QUARTERLY RETURNS 1st quarter March	Home population of previous 30 June Total population of previous 30 June	August	I-3 + part 6‡ I	— Sex, age (5-year groups), marital status
2nd quarter June	Home population at previous 30 June	November	I and hospital regions	Sex and age (5-year groups)
3rd quarter Sept.	Home population at current year, 30 June Estimated total population at current year 30 June Estimated civilian population at current year 30 June	January	I I I	Sex and age (single years to 24 and 5-year groups) Sex and age (5-year groups) Sex and age (5-year groups)
4th quarter Dec.	Home population at current year 30 June	June	I,2,4, part 6§ and hospital regions	Sex and age groups (Areas 1,2, 4:5-year age groups, Area 6: under I year, I-4 years, 5-14 years)

Key to areas covered:

1. England and Wales
2. Region
3. County
4. Conurbation
5. Urban/rural aggregate
6. Local authority area
7. Ward and parish
8. Enumeration district
9. Grid square

NOTES

This table relates only to England and Wales; Scottish publications, omitted for clarity, follow a comparable pattern

* With more than 15,000 population

θ Estimated date

‡ All CBs, MBs, UDs, with an estimated resident population of 25,000 and over at the previous full Census

§ All CBs, City of London, London boroughs and administrative counties

and its home waters, other than on foreign ships, on Census night. This includes:

1. Short- and long-term visitors from abroad whatever their nationality.
2. Armed Forces of the United Kingdom and other nations stationed in this country.
3. Persons on board British, but not foreign, naval vessels at moorings or anchorage or engaged in coastal or fishing voyages.

The enumerated population reflects events which have resulted in a temporary change of address, such as illness, holidays and the requirements of business. A few people will be in transit over Census night and these are enumerated at their place of arrival, which may again not be their home area. The enumerated population of areas within the country will therefore include some whose usual residence is not in those areas, and exclude all those residents who are out of the UK on Census night.

(b) Home or de facto population. Every person in Great Britain and its home waters. The final Home population for Census year for areas within the country (i.e. not the provisional figure based on the previous Census) is derived from the enumerated Census population modified in two ways:

1. adjustment for the period between Census night and 30 June;
2. adjustment, where required, from enumerated to usual place of residence. This is a straightforward operation for the majority of persons in private households who are asked to give their usual address on the Census schedule, where this differs from the one at which they are enumerated. Those people with two or more addresses of equal standing are left to make their own decision as to which is the 'usual' one. For persons in institutions the question raises more problems and will depend in many cases on a judgment by someone as to their likely length of stay. This has been variously dealt with at different times and a full account of changes in definition since 1951 is given in Table 3.

Home population in intercensal years is derived from that of Census year by adjustment for natural increase, estimated net migration and other relevant factors such as demobilisation. This process is considered in detail on pp. 20–24.

(c) Civilian population. Home population less members of the Armed Forces. This is estimated annually only for the UK, England and Wales, Scotland and Northern Ireland.

(d) Total population. Civilian population and members of HM Armed Forces wherever stationed. The total is therefore derived from Home population less members of Armed Forces other than those of this country plus British Armed Forces from this country who are abroad. Civilian British nationals out of this country cannot for practical reasons be included. However, in 1951 when so many British nationals were still abroad as a result of postwar commitments a count was made of UK-based members of the Armed Forces abroad with their civilian staff, families, and any other attached personnel such as welfare workers, by their commanding officers. In addition, UK-based personnel attached to Foreign Office establishments abroad were also enumerated by the Foreign Office, while information on British crews serving in seagoing vessels registered in the UK, providing they had previously been included in a British Census, was supplied by the Registrar of Shipping and Seamen. These totals were published in an Appendix to the General Tables of the 1951 Census and could be used to provide a more accurate estimate of total population. Total population is again only estimated for the UK, England and Wales, Scotland and Northern Ireland. The difference between Total and Home population has become less over time. In 1951 the ratio between the two was 1.004, in 1968, 1.002.[1]

Area definitions

All areas defined for population data purposes within the national boundary are based on aggregations of local authorities, or of wards or parishes within local authority areas.

7

(a) Standard Regions, and regional subdivisions (see pp. 132–134 for authorities within Regions).

The largest areas into which Great Britain is divided are the Standard Regions. Between 1951 and 1965 nine Standard Regions were defined in England and two in Wales; after 1965 the number of Regions in England was reduced to eight. In Scotland the equivalent areas are four geographical divisions. In 1966 Economic Planning Regions were defined and these correspond to the Standard Regions with the exception of Poole, which was placed in the Southern Region, though within the South West Regional Economic Planning Council. The major change from the pre-1966 Regions was the inclusion of Greater London with the South East Regions but within this Region, a division is generally made into the Greater London Council Area, which replaced the Greater London conurbation in 1965, the Outer Metropolitan Area and the remainder. Regional economic planning subdivisions were defined in 1968.

Subdivisions in Scotland are partly geographical and partly industrial, separating crofting counties in the North and border counties in the Southern Divisions.

(b) Conurbations (see pp. 135–137 for authorities included), *Conurbation divisions and subdivisions and conurbation centre.* The term 'conurbation' was first introduced by the Registrar General at the time of the 1951 Census of Population, though the word itself was first suggested at the beginning of the century by Patrick Geddes,[2] to describe the concentrations of population within the country, around the great cities. In the context of government statistics, it is used to describe areas more limited in size which were defined by an interdepartmental committee in 1950 'as a means of securing uniformity and comparability in statistics published by Government Departments in the United Kingdom'. In their report they stated that 'conurbation is the word used to describe those areas of urban development where a number of separate towns have grown into each other and become linked by such factors as a common industrial or business interest or a

common centre of shopping, education, etc. The conurbations are each made up of a collection of complete local authority areas.'[3]

The six English conurbations are Greater London, West Midlands, South East Lancashire, Merseyside, Tyneside and West Yorkshire. Revisions to the local authorities within the Greater London and West Midlands conurbations were made in 1969, but the remainder are the same. In Scotland only one conurbation has been defined, the Central Clydeside conurbation.

A special *Conurbation* volume was produced from 1951 Census data for England and Wales, an innovation not repeated in subsequent years. In this volume, an attempt was made to facilitate comparison between conurbations by forming conurbation divisions and subdivisions on the basis of local authority areas, wards and parishes. However, as differing circumstances had affected the definition of these areas, the number of divisions varied between conurbations, and it was recommended that comparison should be within rather than between them.

The aim was to define relatively homogeneous zones, from the central administrative and commercial area through belts of differing types of development, except in West Yorkshire where economic criteria were used.[4] Within the divisions, further breakdowns were made into subdivisions. In the Conurbation volume of 1951, a description of the general demographic characteristics of the divisions and subdivisions is given before the section relating to the conurbation of which they form part.

An area related to the conurbation which has been used since 1961 is the *conurbation centre*. This was defined as a central area identified in each of the six conurbations except West Yorkshire containing the principal concentration of administrative and commercial offices, major shopping streets, theatres, cinemas and dance halls, public buildings, hotels, special areas and precincts (e.g. university, cathedral and legal) and main railway coach terminal. It is characterised by relatively low residential population, by a large concentration of employment, involving journey to work, and often by traffic congestion and car parking problems.[5]

Maps illustrating the conurbation centres, which are based on groups of enumeration districts, are provided in the appropriate County Reports.

(c) Urban and rural aggregates. In the 1961 and later Census volumes for England and Wales data are aggregated into groups of local authority areas according to their type and size. Five divisions are made:

1. Conurbations
2. Urban areas (Boroughs and Urban districts as defined by Local Government Acts) with populations of 100,000 or more
3. Urban areas with populations of 50,000 and less than 100,000
4. Urban areas with populations of less than 50,000
5. Rural districts.

These divisions are also used in the Registrar General's other statistical publications after this date.

In Scotland the equivalent divisions are named Burghal/Landward Areas, as follows:

1. Conurbation (Central Clydeside)
2. Burghal areas with a population of 100,000 or more
3. Burghal areas with a population of 10,000 and less than 100,000
4. Burghal areas with a population of less than 10,000
5. Landward areas.

Areas for which Census data are made available

Special purchases of Census data may be made for small areas which allow greater flexibility than local government areas.

(d) The enumeration district and Ward Library data. A basic area for which data have been made available by the Registrar General since 1951 is the enumeration district. This is the area allocated to an enumerator at the Census within which he is responsible for the distribution and collection of Census schedules. No one district belongs to more than one local authority or more than one ward, but occasionally it contains two or more parishes where the population is low. 'Special' enumeration districts consist of one large establishment such as a prison, hospital or ship.

The boundaries of enumeration districts were originally drawn up by the Census Officers, but in 1961 this work was done by General Register Office (G.R.O.) staff.[6] In 1966 and 1971 interested bodies were invited to cooperate in drawing enumeration district boundaries—in particular, local planning departments with knowledge of new housing development were able to ensure that the population within the districts approached the population standard set by the GRO.

Until 1951 no use was made of the data for individual enumeration districts outside the GRO, where they were aggregated into totals at the various levels required. A change of policy was achieved after the 1951 Census, however, when the Registrar General agreed to provide statistical counts for enumeration districts combined into thirty-five tracts dividing Oxford into areas whose boundaries were drawn 'to ensure that the population in each tract is as homogeneous in social and economic characteristics as possible, while keeping the numbers large enough to protect the anonymity of the smallest group within it'.[7] It was agreed that there should be continuity of the tract areas in further Censuses to allow comparative studies.

The Oxford Census tract material led directly to a request by other bodies for similar statistics to be made available and in 1961 the Registrar General agreed to do this, at a charge, by providing counts for enumeration districts either in the form of tabulations or on punched cards. Entitled *Ward Library* data, the offer was taken up by some of the larger local authorities and a number of universities. By 1966 its value was more generally recognised, particularly in relation to the growth of new and expanded towns, and the redevelopment of central areas, and in this year and 1971 Ward Library statistics were again made available, subject to confidentiality restraints made necessary by smaller numbers in the enumeration districts, in the form of tabulations or on magnetic tape.

In 1961 enumeration districts in urban areas contained 250–300 households, and a population of approximately 1,000; rural enumeration districts contained fewer. In 1966 three or four 1961 enumeration districts were combined except where gross changes in population in the intervening period led to a different arrangement, in order to achieve the aim of about 1,000 households within each enumeration district. It was not practical to retain the 1961 or 1966 boundaries for the 1971 Census and the great majority were redrawn so that the number of households in an enumeration district was reduced to about 150.

(e) *The National Grid Square*. In 1971 a further step was taken in recognition of the value of small area analysis. The great disadvantage of enumeration districts for this purpose is that their boundaries necessarily change from one census to another in areas where large increases or decreases of population have occurred,[8] so that those areas of particular interest because of a change in density have been those most likely to be lost. The grid square unit is permanent and so overcomes this difficulty. In 1971 a geocode based on National Grid coordinate references, was provided for every residential place of enumeration where up to date large-scale Ordnance Survey maps were available; the areas not covered in this way include less than 10 per cent of the population. Both 100m grid square references and 1m coordinate references can be used to aggregate data within areas defined either by the Office of Population Censuses and Surveys (OPCS) or other users, always subject to the need to protect confidentiality. Referencing co-ordinates for enumeration districts will be included in the Ward Library data.

Such data will be provided after the Ward Library data and are likely to be expensive to buy. The extent of their use will no doubt govern the future policy of the OPCS—it is likely to be of particular value in computer mapping, and in time may well become the basic unit in all data collection.

Boundary changes

Boundary changes usually arise at local authority level and can cause difficulty in making comparisons over time. In the population tables of the Census volumes, areas whose boundaries have changed since the preceding Census are indicated.

Boundary changes may be small in size but often affect population numbers disproportionately, as the reason for a boundary extension is commonly the development of an overspill estate beyond the boundary of the overspilling authority which then claims the area as its own. In more recent years, expanded towns may result in large additions of acreage, and eventually large increases of population, while New Towns usually obtain their acreage from a number of established, often rural, authorities.

On the other hand, static boundaries do not imply a static position as regards population, and the movement out of cities to peripheral areas which has been such a feature of postwar development often means that the boundary has little meaning except for rating purposes. The concept of the city region or conurbation first recognised by the Registrar General in the 1951 Census, does to some extent provide a means of assessing population change unlimited by artificial boundaries, but this type of redistribution is now considerably more widespread than within the six great conurbations.

Information concerning boundary changes—the area and estimated population involved—is usually published in the Registrar General's *Quarterly Returns* for June and December, and the *Annual Statistical Review,* Part II. Details of intercensal changes are also given in the Census County Reports.

The need for confidentiality

The GRO and OPCS have always believed that the need to preserve the anonymity of respondents is paramount. This has posed some problems in the publication of material for small areas, particularly where enumeration has been on a sample basis. Data from the 1966 Sample Census were therefore only published outside the Ward Library for local authority areas with a population expected to be more than 15,000 on Census day.

THE FORM OF SOURCE PUBLICATIONS

Census publications

The bulk of Census material is published in County Reports and volumes concerned with special topics. The first contains basic demographic data including population for areas within each county down to ward level. Many data other than counts of population are collected at the Census, and these will be examined in the following chapters, but the general discussion which follows in this chapter, concerning the organisation and reliability of the Census, is equally relevant to all topics.

In order to provide as early information as possible from the Census special arrangements have been made to supply advance estimates of the population count and a limited number of other data. These, with the methods used to obtain them, have varied to some extent at each Census since 1951.

(a) Preliminary Census Reports: 1951, 1961, 1971. A Preliminary Report has been produced a few months after each postwar Census except that of 1966, giving a provisional count of population by sex, and after 1951 of private households and dwellings down to local authority area level. The procedure for deriving these figures is different from that of the later information, for they are obtained from records made by the enumerators themselves when the schedule is delivered, resulting in a total of the number of persons by sex in each household and dwelling for their own enumeration district. In 1951 it was the responsibility of the Census Officers to provide a total for their area from these records which was sent to the GRO, and in this year the Preliminary Report was published only three months after Census day. In 1961 the enumerators were provided with sensitised cards for their summaries which were used for 'mark sense' machine punching. By unsurpassed (and no doubt unsurpassable) efforts the 1961 Preliminary Report came out only six weeks after Census Day.

Difficulties had arisen in the use of the report card, however, and this experiment was not repeated. Instead, in 1966 summary sheets were filled in and totals forwarded to the GRO as in 1951. No Preliminary Report for 1966 was published because difficulties arose related to the combination of the 10 per cent sample of private households and 100 per cent enumeration of institutions. There were misunderstandings among Census Officers and enumerators concerning their inclusion in the abstracts of records to be used for the preliminary analysis and the time which would have been required to make corrections was too great for the work to be worth while. The moral has been drawn by Gray and Gee of the Social Survey Division that 'variable sampling fractions are sometimes necessary but always dangerous'.[9]

In 1971 two forms of preliminary analysis were made. The first corresponded with those of previous Census years, prepared from enumerators' totals for their districts. From these, counts of population by sex were obtained as usual and published less than four months after Census Day.

(b) Advance analyses, 1971. In order to provide additional information at an early date, Advanced Analyses were prepared after the 1971 Census from special documents readable by ICL Universal Document Readers, on line to the OPCS's 1904A computer. Enumerators abstracted information from the completed schedule relating to sex, age, marital status, country of birth, parents' country of birth and economic activity. Apart from country of birth, this was published in England and Wales only for local authority areas with a population of more than 15,000; errors in transcription prevented the publication of country of birth data at lower than national level and of household size altogether.

The Advanced Analyses were published in the form of county leaflets, the first available eight months after Census day, the last expected about three months after the first. In Scotland, equivalent information was published as a second Preliminary Report, and provided for counties, cities, large burghs and some larger county districts. As well as enumerated population, resident populations of recently proposed new local government regions and districts were given.

(c) The 1 per cent sample : 1951, 1971. In 1951 a 1 per cent sample of schedules was selected and used to produce a complete range of Census data within fifteen months. The need for such information was probably greater in 1951 than at previous Censuses, for there

was a gap of twenty years to cover, only partly filled by the National Register, within which great changes had occurred.

The innovation was not repeated in 1961, perhaps because for the first time a computer was used in place of punched card machines, and it was believed that this would lead to much speedier processing. In the event, a number of unexpected circumstances led to considerable delay, but the experience gained led to a greatly improved processing time for 1966 data. However, although the basic demographic data were available within a relatively short period after the 1961 and 1966 Censuses, publication of data on special topics such as migration, occupation, industry, journey to work and so on, which followed the county reports, continued for a further two years. To reduce this gap a 1 per cent sample of schedules was again taken in 1971, linked in this case to a voluntary income enquiry.

Publication of the annual estimates

The annual mid-year estimates of the Home population of England and Wales and of Scotland, standard regions, rural and urban aggregates, conurbations and local authority areas first appear in provisional form in the Registrar General's *Annual Estimates of Population,* available about the start of the following year. They are also published for certain areas (see Table 1) in the *Quarterly Returns,* appearing first for the larger areas in the December returns (published usually during March) and for the larger of the local authorities in the following March quarter, which also has estimates of the Total population of England and Wales.

The estimates appear also in the *Annual Statistical Review,* Parts I and II for all areas down to local authorities (Table 1). These are usually published about twenty-one months after the mid-year to which the estimates relate. Part I, the *Medical Volume,* contains additional information on causes of death; Part II, the *Population Volume* (termed the *Civil Volume* until 1957), contains additional information on fertility rates.

Part III of the Review is a *Commentary Volume* containing descriptions of various aspects of collection and estimation of the data provided in the first two parts, and additional tabulations. The time-lag between the *Commentary Volume* and the others has gradually increased and is now over two years.

The Electoral Register

The Electoral Register is compiled annually and is used for any election occurring in the period 16 February to 15 February of the following year, although qualification for inclusion relates to the previous October. Each register covers a polling district within a constituency and lists all those within the area eligible to vote there. A complete set is available in the British Museum, but they may also be seen or purchased at the Town Clerk's or County Clerk's office in the authority to which they relate. The main register lists those entitled to vote currently, or reaching the age at which they are entitled to vote, the 'B' list those who are on the current register who were not on the previous one and the 'C' list those who were on the previous register but not on the current one.

A detailed description of the Electoral Register is given in chapter 5, with a discussion of its use as a sampling frame. Compared with the Census, its reliability is low but it provides a useful indication of the general magnitude of large-scale changes in adult population, and it can be used in this way independently of administrative boundaries, for any size of area. Ward totals from the Electoral Registers are usually published in the local authorities' municipal year book, and often in the Report of the Medical Officer of Health. In addition, totals for counties and constituencies are published in the Registrar General's *Annual Statistical Review*, Part II and can be obtained in advance from the OPCS (Electoral Statistics Branch, Titchfield) for a small price.

THE COLLECTION AND ESTIMATION OF POPULATION DATA

The degree of reliability which may be attached to any set of figures must be related to a large extent to the way in which the figures have been obtained. In this section, therefore, those factors concerned in the collection or estimation of population figures most likely to affect their reliability are considered.

The Census enumeration

As the quantity of information collected at the Census has grown, the need for careful control of its quality has become more appreciated and preparatory work has increased. The 1951 *General Report* states that the main preparation for the 1951 Census began in 1949. Apart from the design and preparation of schedules and publicity arrangements, this largely consisted of the appointment of Census Officers—with few exceptions Registrars or persons associated with the registration services, who had the following duties:

1. delineation of enumeration district boundaries and identification of 'special' enumeration districts—large non-private establishments in their area;
2. selection and appointment of enumerators;
3. instructing enumerators by ensuring their familiarity with the area to be covered and providing them with their instructions in the form of an enumeration book produced at the GRO, schedules, record cards and so on.

It was the enumerators' own responsibility to 'make himself fully conversant with his instructions . . . printed in the Enumeration Book'.[10]

The *General Report* of the 1961 Census states that preparation began for this Census in 1957—a period twice as long as for the previous one. This additional time was required largely because of the introduction of multiphase sampling at the time of enumeration and also because processing was to be by computer for the first time in this country, an innovation for which many changes in procedure were necessary. A third reason was that enumeration district boundaries were this time drawn by GRO staff rather than by Census Officers, in order to eliminate the difficulties caused by the delay in completing this work which had occurred in 1951. This procedure has been followed since, and will almost certainly be followed in the future.

The introduction of sampling at enumeration level, which in 1961 involved the selection of one in ten households to provide supplementary information, led to some changes in organisation. More time was spent on instruction and enumerators were briefed by their Census Officers, who had themselves been instructed by the GRO on procedure, though for the great majority this was again done by information in documentary form rather than by personal contacts with GRO staff. The mechanics of the sampling was shared by the GRO and the Census Officers, and the latter therefore retained the greater part of the responsibility for distribution and collection of schedules, though in the preparatory work there was some move towards centralised direction.

The reliability of the results of this Census will be discussed in more detail in the following chapter; here it will be sufficient to note that the need for rigorous adherence to the sampling procedure laid down by the GRO was not appreciated by many enumerators and probably Census Officers also. When a decision was taken to conduct a census in 1966 entirely on a sample basis, plans were made for greatly improved training at all levels. Senior instructors trained at the GRO organised weekend courses for Census Officers who were then able to instruct their enumerators and deal adequately with difficulties arising. The sample addresses of private households and small non-private establishments were provided by the GRO who also selected the samples of residents in large establishments which were mostly enumerated on a 100 per cent basis.

In preparation for the 1966 Census, therefore, there was a further move towards centralised control as far as this was practical. The general principles used in training then were followed again in 1971, though training procedures used by the Census Officers for the enumerators were more standardised, by means of training packages provided by the OPCS containing notes, display charts, practical exercises and mock interviews. (The change from GRO to OPCS occurred during this period, in 1970.) Two television training programmes were also provided by the BBC.[11] Thus 1971 saw further steps in the reduction of the Census Officer's responsibility for procedures in the field both in training and in sample selection, for in this Census, although certain information was analysed on a sample basis, selection of the sample was made at the GRO after a full enumeration throughout the country.

Annual estimations of population

Three major elements are involved in the annual calculation of population estimates from Census figures relating to usual residence, apart from the small adjustment from Census night to 30 June. These are:

1. natural increase
2. migration
3. movement of the armed forces.

The annual mid-year estimates are calculated in a provisional form in October of the year to which they relate. Fresh evidence after November which entails revision of the estimates is usually incorporated in the subsequent years' estimates, but an exception is made for new Census figures which lead to new estimates published for the same year. However, Census population adjusted to usual residence as opposed to the enumerated counts published in the *Preliminary Report* from enumerator's records, is required for areas within the country, and until 1971 these had not been computed until more than a year after the Census enumeration. In the meantime, provisional figures were published for Census year, calculated on the same basis as other intercensal estimates. As errors inevitably accumulate in this intercensal period, particularly in relation to local authority areas, where they are most dependent on assessments of internal migration, the revision may be of some size.

Natural increase. Of the three main components of population change, natural increase is the one most accurately known. Registration of births and deaths has been compulsory since 1874 and it is unlikely that, except in a negligible number of cases, they are not recorded. However, even here there are two factors which may lead to temporary inaccuracy. A period of forty-two days is allowed for birth registration and five days for registration of death. These 'registrations' must then, where necessary, be allocated to the place of usual residence as 'occurrences', an adjustment affecting a significant proportion, as many births and deaths take place in ·hospitals which may well be in a different local authority from the home address. The redistribution for the quarter April to June is not completed by October, and so 'occurrences' for this period must themselves be estimated.

Migration. The migration constituent is difficult to assess accurately, expecially for smaller areas, and this may at times lead to gross inaccuracies. For the country as a whole, only figures for external migration are required, but within the country internal migration is an additional factor. The assessment of these two types of movement will be considered in turn.

External migration. The first need here is to distinguish migrant from visitor and this must depend largely on the stated intentions of the person concerned. In a proportion of cases this may well be in error, through a change in intention.

The definition of external migrant used by the Registrar General for estimating this component of the population is a person who declares his intention of staying in the United Kingdom or abroad—the first as immigrant, the second as emigrant—for an unbroken period of twelve months or more.[12] This differs slightly from the definition recommended by the International Statistical Institute, which adds a previous residence of at least one year as a requirement. The two variations may be compared with the Census definition of 1961 which is 'a person whose residence twelve months before Census day was different from that on Census day'.[13] In taking no account of the intended length of stay, the Census definition will exclude a number of persons identified as migrants in the previous definitions. Additionally, the Census is unable to provide data concerning external emigrants.

Census data are, therefore, not used to estimate the total size of net external migration other than providing guidance on the number of migrants from southern Ireland, but they do provide information on the distribution of immigrants within the country and on the composition of immigrant households, and other demographic characteristics.

Since 1964, the Registrar General's estimates of the number of external migrants other than those to and from Ireland, have been based on the International Passenger Survey, a running sample survey conducted by the OPCS Social Survey Division.[14] Before this time some estimate was obtained from passports and records of shipping and airline companies, but as the volume of movement grew those sources became inadequate, while the importance of accurate information increased.

The International Passenger Survey obtains its data by interviewing a random sample of sea and air passengers as they enter or leave the United Kingdom, other than those travelling to and from southern Ireland. The samples taken are relatively small, the proportion of passengers selected varying according to the total number involved in the particular type of movement. It is therefore highest for the long sea and air routes, and lowest for the short routes in summer. Little information is obtained in addition to that on the country of origin or destination, but age, sex, marital status and usual occupation are obtained.

Births to external migrants after arrival and their deaths are, of course, included with those of the resident population as part of the figure of natural increase.

Internal migration. While population estimates for the United Kingdom require information only concerning external migrants, those for smaller areas require in addition estimates of internal migration.

Since the National Register terminated in 1953, no records of internal movement have been kept in this country, and estimates rely mainly on two sources, the Electoral Register and the Housing Returns.

The form of registration for electoral purposes is described in chapter 5. The main registers with the B and C lists give a reasonably good indication of major changes in population occurring up to October of the year for which the estimates are made.

Large-scale changes after this month and before the following June will be missed. They must also clearly be augmented by estimates of the population too young to appear in them and again this may present difficulty during periods of substantial change.

Such omissions may be at least partly covered by the Housing Development Returns, submitted voluntarily by most local authorities, though some do not respond. These provide data concerning new housing, and demolished dwellings and so indicate areas of growth or decline. Overspill housing schemes, which are controlled closely by the local authority concerned, are reported with a greater degree of accuracy than development in the private sector. Guidance is also obtained from the annual returns of institutions, such as prisons, hospitals, schools, etc., concerning changes in their resident population, again indicating areas of substantial growth or contraction.

Armed forces. The last component taken into account in mid-year estimations is the distribution of the armed forces. The overall number stationed within the United Kingdom and abroad can be provided with reasonable accuracy at a particular time, but break-downs within this area can only be assessed approximately. Similarly the number of men and women demobilised within each area is not available and so the total leaving the armed forces is allocated to each area in the same proportion as men and women of the same age group in the civilian population.

The gain in population to an area as a result of demobilisation is some part of the residual obtained when the appropriate natural increase is deducted from the difference in population at two periods of time. The greater part represents net migration but the proportion taken up by demobilisation will clearly vary from one year to another. In the immediate postwar years it was a highly significant factor, but by the mid-1950s it had shrunk, though increasing a little again in the early 1960s.

One other factor associated with the armed forces which concerns Total population, that is all United Kingdom citizens at home or abroad, is that of deaths occurring overseas. However, in times of peace the numbers involved are so small that it is not considered necessary to incorporate them. They are almost certainly smaller in normal times than the number of deaths of UK businessmen or other visitors abroad, which is also ignored.

THE RELIABILITY OF POPULATION ESTIMATES

The reliability of the mid-year estimates depends, among other things, on the accuracy of the Census count. This is examined by the Registrar General and analysed, as far as population is concerned, in his Statistical Review Commentary. A final review is made in the *General Report,* the last *Report* of the Census series to be published. From 1951, the checks made have become increasingly rigorous.

Since the organisation of the Census was placed in the hands of the Registrar General in 1841, the enumeration has been carried out carefully, and great efforts are made to reach every member of the population. It is believed that in the more recent Censuses, with the possible exception of 1971, when the effect of a campaign against compulsory registration had as yet unknown results, few omissions occur. Those that do, however, are likely to be concentrated in certain sections of the population—immigrants and residents in highly multi-occupied dwellings for whose registration a landlord may be responsible, are the most obvious groups. Some homeless may also be missed, although it seems probable that the majority are located by the police. In overall terms, therefore, the omissions are probably negligible, but among certain subgroups in the larger cities they may be of more consequence.

So far as the population count is concerned, a comparison with the mid-year estimate for Census year gives a useful indication of inaccuracy on one side or the other and whether there is need for a more detailed analysis to discover where the discrepancy has arisen. It must be remembered, however, that a substantial portion of the simple difference between the two totals may be due to differences in definition.

1951. It was not possible to validate the 1951 Census population by such a comparison, because the mid-year estimates for this year differed in origin from those in other intercensal periods. Because of wartime conditions, no Census was held in 1941, and between 1939 and 1951 mid-year estimates were based on the National Register, a continuous register of civilians required for the issue of ration books. The complication of conscription, with movement in and out of the armed forces meant that the migration component was particularly difficult to assess and depended on a number of assumptions.

The enumerated Census population of 1951 was less than the expected population based on mid-year estimates by 134,000, but in the *General Report* it is stated that the likelihood of under-estimation in the Census is 'quite trivial'.[15] It seemed most likely that errors arising in the estimated 'expected' population lay in the armed forces element.

1961. Mid-year estimates for 1960 and 1961 agreed closely with the 100 per cent enumerated Census population, and the difference between the expected population based on these figures and the Census count was only 54,000. However, in the *General Report* a warning is given that the closeness of the figures does not neces-sarily validate either. It is suggested that an underestimation of net migration in the intercensal period and an underenumeration of some immigrant groups could have led to similar understatement in both cases.[16]

Because of the fear that in fact there had been such under-estimation, particularly in relation to the heavy Commonwealth immigration which had occurred in the period, a comparison was made, of which there is an account in the *General Report,* between the mid-year estimates and Census resident population of a number of Metropolitan Boroughs where West Indians were known to be concentrated. These again showed a close correspondence and it is concluded that although some underenumeration is probable, particularly of immigrants in multi-occupied buildings, it was not as great as had been suggested.

After the 1961 Census, partly because of the sampling element in this Census, more elaborate checks of all the information collected were devised, than ever before. Most important of all was a post-enumeration survey[17] carried out in mid-May by selected enumerators who visited 2,500 plots throughout England and Wales, each containing about 20 households. No similar survey was made in Scotland.

Part of the survey was devised to check on coverage[18] and it suggested a net under-enumeration of 0·2 per 1000. (95 per cent confidence limits are ± 0·3 per 1,000.) People not counted amounted to approximately 1·6 per 1,000, and duplication to approximately 1·4 per 1,000. It was found that both types of error were highest in county boroughs and municipal boroughs and lowest in rural districts.

It will be remembered that in 1961 selection of the 10 per cent sample for special topics was very largely the responsibility of the enumerator. In the case of private households, a 1 in 10 selection of households was planned, and in non-private households a 1 in 10 selection of individuals. The bias which arose in this sample affected all aspects of the data collected, but that least affected was the number of persons in the sample which closely approached 10 per cent of the total population. Bias will therefore be considered in detail in the following chapter, together with a discussion of the role of the enumerator (see chapter 2).

The total number of persons actually selected in fact exceeded the expected total by only 0·5 per cent, a difference well within the variation to be expected in random sampling. At enumeration district level, there was a marked preponderance of districts where too large a sample was taken.

In non-private households, there was a net 8 per cent deficiency in the sample taken from hotels and boarding houses resulting from a 15 per cent deficiency among guests (1·9 per cent for resident as opposed to visitor guests) and a 7 per cent excess of managers, their staff and relatives, probably as a result of substitution. The GRO points out that the bias factors they have provided take no account of this distortion. In other types of non-private household, there was a net surplus of about 1 per cent, and although again the sample in most cases contained excess of staff, it is not considered that the differences here are serious.

1966. A *General Report* assessing the 1966 10 per cent sample Census results has not yet been published, but a brief evaluation is available in the *Statistical Review Commentary* for 1967. As the age distribution of the population is of particular importance to the intercensal national estimates, this aspect of the Sample Census has been examined in detail. The number of children below the age of 5 years is known with some accuracy from birth registrations and those of 5–15 years from school records. Comparison suggests underenumeration in both these groups, in part perhaps through underenumeration of households containing more than six persons, where a second Census Schedule would be required. Other unspecified sources suggest underenumeration of men aged 20–49 years.

Apart from the special case of large households, underenumeration in this Census can largely be ascribed to the inadequacy of the sampling frame. This frame was primarily based on the lists of household addresses available from the full 1961 Census, and these appear to have been reliable. It was in the addition of dwellings constructed since that time from rating lists that the deficiencies largely occurred. The amount of underestimation was therefore not evenly spread throughout the country but was especially high in areas with large-scale recent development, in particular Greater London and the larger urban areas.

As a result of this evaluation, revisions were made to the mid-year estimates for 1966 which took the Census under estimation into account. The enumerated population was increased by more than 750,000 in total, but the new estimates were lower by 90,000 than the old.[19] The comment is made in the *Statistical Review* that the result of the full 1971 Census will be 'exceptionally important in giving the basis for a complete reappraisal of the accuracy of the estimates of population change over the decade since 1961'.[20]

1971. To quote from *Statistical News,* no. 16 (p. 16): 'The 1971 Census was carried out to the accompaniment of an unprecedented amount of publicity and discussion largely concerned with the confidentiality of returns', and it was generally feared that this might lead to a substantial drop from the usual almost complete enumeration. The immediate cause of concern appears to have arisen from the insertion of questions concerning ethnic origin, in particular to the birthplace of parents. However, there seems little doubt that use was made of the general ignorance of the purpose to which Census data are put and easily aroused fears of additional harassment among the immigrant population, to provide publicity for a number of organisations and individuals.

In the event 177,000 Census returns were made directly to the OPCS rather than to the enumerators, some incomplete. A rather higher than usual number of refusals also occurred. The direct returns led to at least two months' delay in the publication of the *Preliminary Report* largely because of the checks to be made and missing information to be obtained. It can only be hoped that a final evaluation will show the effect on the data to have been negligible.

Other Census topics 2

A general survey of the organisation of the Census, and variations in the form it has taken since the war has been made in the preceding chapter. Aspects such as reliability have been considered largely as they relate to population data. In this chapter, other Census topics are reviewed, with a closer look at changes in definition, reliability and sample bias—factors which only marginally affect the basic count of population.

A very detailed account of the census in more recent years, the information collected and the 'concepts which form the basis of Census questions' has been given by Benjamin in an SSRC publication.[1] There will be no attempt here to look at these particular aspects in such detail, but a list of subjects covered in postwar censuses is given in Table 2, with the census years in which they appear and the level at which they are tabulated.

PROBLEMS OF INTERPRETATION

Definitions

Unlike population, where only marginal changes in definition can arise, mainly concerning the inclusion or not of non-residents and members of the armed forces, most Census topics can be varied to a considerable extent. Such variation is not necessarily due to an arbitrary decision that an improvement can be made, for the importance of comparability between Censuses is well recognised today. Few of the earlier nineteenth-century Censuses provided a basis for comparison; although some subjects such as occupation have appeared in some form in every Census since the first in 1801,

TABLE 2
Postwar Census topics

Subject	Year appearing	Level tabulated %	Additional specifications
I. PERSONAL CHARACTERISTICS			
Sex, Age, Marital status, Relationship to head of household, Usual residence	All	100 except 1966 10% Sample	
Date of marriage	1951	100	Married women under age 50, present and first marriage
	1961	100	All married women, present and first marriage
	1971	10	Married, widowed or divorced women under age 60, first marriage only
Date marriage ended	1961	100	Widowed, divorced, more than once married—first marriage only
	1971	10	As 1961, under age 60 only
Number of children	1951	100	Born alive to married women under age 50
	1961	100	Born alive to married, widowed, divorced women
	1971	100	As 1961 under age 60
Children born in previous 12 months	1951	100	Live to married women under age 50
	1961	100	Live to all married, widowed, divorced women
	1971	10	As 1961, to women under 60
Birthdate of all children born alive	1971	100	To all married, widowed and divorced women under age 60
Birthplace	1951	100	County and town or parish if born in UK
	1961	100	Country only in England and Wales; county in Scotland
	1966	10	As 1951 related to mother's usual residence
	1971	100	Country only
Nationality	1951	100	If British, by what right
	1961	100	If citizen of Commonwealth, state citizenship; if of UK and Colonies, by what right?

TABLE 2 *(cont'd)*

Year of entry into UK (tabulated for entry after 1960)	1971	100	Country of origin only
Birthplace of parents	1971	100	Country only
Welsh-speaking	1951	100	in Wales and Monmouthshire
	1961	100	in Wales only
Gaelic-speaking	1961	100	in Scotland only
Persons absent on Census night usually in household	1961	10	Relationship to head, sex, age, marital status, address on Census night
	1966	10	Address on Census night
	1971	10	As 1961 and economic activity

2. HOUSEHOLD AND DWELLING CHARACTERISTICS

No. of households in dwelling	All*	100 except 1966 10% Sample	
Tenure‡	1961	100	
	1966	10	
	1971	100	
Number of rooms	1951*	100	
	1961*	100	
	1966	10	Kitchen and scullery enumerated separately, and whether used for meals
	1971	100	Shared rooms enumerated separately by enumerator
Arrangements: Cooking stove or range	1951*	100	Exclusive use, shared or none
	1961*	100	Combined with sink, whether shared or in shared dwelling
	1966*	10	Whether exclusive use in shared dwelling
	1971	100	With oven, exclusive use, shared or none
Kitchen sink	1951*	100	Exclusive use, shared or none
	1961*	100	Combined with stove, whether shared or in shared dwelling
	1966*	10	Whether exclusive use in shared dwelling
	1971	100	Whether connected to water supply and waste pipe, exclusive use, shared or none
Piped water supply inside house: cold	1951	100	Exclusive use, shared or none
	1961	100	Sole use, shared or none
	1971	100	With waste pipe, connected to kitchen sink, fixed bath or shower

TABLE 2 *(cont'd)*

Piped water supply inside house: hot	1961	100	Sole use, shared or none
	1966	10	As 1961
	1971	100	As 1961
WC	1951	100	Exclusive use, shared or none
	1961	100	Sole use, shared or none in building
	1966	10	As 1961, flush toilet with entrance outside building
	1971	100	As 1961, flush toilet, entrance inside or outside
Fixed bath	1951	100	Exclusive use, shared or none
	1961	100	Sole use, shared or none
	1966	10	As 1961 within building
	1971	100	As 1961, connected to water supply and waste pipe
Fixed shower	1966	10	
	1971	100	Alternative to fixed bath

3. EDUCATION

Terminal education age	1951	100	
	1961	10	
Type of educational establishment attended at time of Census	1951	100	Full time or part time
Qualifications	1961	10	In science or technology
	1966	10	Major subjects
	1971	10	(a) A level GCE or equivalent§
			(b) ONC or OND
			(c) HNC or HND
			(d) Nursing or teaching qualification
			(e) Degree, diploma, etc.
			(f) Other professional qualification
			All excluding persons under 18 years old and over 70 years if retired
			(c)-(f)-main subjects and awarding institution

4. MIGRATION

Usual address 1 year previously	1961	10	
	1966	10	
	1971	10	
Usual address 5 years previously	1966	10	
	1971	10	

TABLE 2 *(cont'd)*

5. EMPLOYMENT			
Occupation	⎫	1951:100	Incl. apprentice, student, etc.
Occupational status	⎬ All	1961,1966,	Applies to most recent work if
Industry		1971:10	unemployed or retired
Place of work	⎭		(Main employment specified in 1971)
Part-time work	1951	100	
	1961	10	No. of hours worked prev. week; males—last full-time employment
	1966	10	No. of hours worked prev. week
Hours per week usually worked	1971	10	Excluding overtime and meal breaks
Out of employment	1951	100	
	1961	10	Previous week, specified if sick
	1966	10	Previous week, previous 12 months, previous Monday (If latter whether registered at Exchange)
	1971	10	Previous week, reason for non-employment
Transport to work	1966	10	Normally, for longest part by distance
	1971	10	As 1966
Jobs additional to principal occupation	1966	10	
Occupation 1 year previously	1971	10	
6. CARS AND GARAGING			
Number of cars owned or used exclusively	1966	10	Including vans used as private vehicle
	1971	10	Including vans not used solely for carriage of goods
Overnight storage	1966	10	

* Information provided by enumerator
‡ Owner occupied, rented, etc.
§ HSC, Higher grade SCE, Higher grade SLC

only the breakdown of population into sex and age (when obtained) can be said to be truly comparable throughout.

The *General Report* of 1961 points out[2] that there are a number of reasons for non-comparability apart from the understandable wish to improve; many of these are beyond the control of the Census office. The main factors concerned are of three types:

1. *Administrative changes,* for example:

(a) Changes in the school-leaving age affect all data concerned with education, employment, economic status and industry.

(b) Changes in sovereignty affect tabulations by birthplace where countries of origin are usually combined within similarly administered groups, such as colonies and Commonwealth countries. The change from British nationality to Commonwealth citizenship between 1951 and 1961 was an additional complication.

2. *Changes over time* not reflected in administrative change, for example:

(a) Birthplace tables provide less and less accurate information concerning the distribution of ethnic groups as the number of second and third generation immigrants increases.

(b) The development of new types of industry leads to the reduction and eventual disappearance of older ones, and with them certain occupations. The growth of light engineering and the electronics industry is a dramatic example in postwar years of the introduction of a new range of occupations. There has, too, been a reduction in the number of unskilled occupations and an increase in those requiring at least a minimum of training. These and similar trends have led to changes in the classification of industry and occupation in postwar years.

(c) Changes in the character of occupations or in the nature of duties performed may occur while the same name is retained. This is associated to some extent with the previous example, though often a result of broader economic trends. Domestic service is an example here.

3. *Changes introduced to improve the quality of the analysis made.*
Such changes are introduced for a number of reasons including:

(a) Ambiguity, which has led to differences in interpretation between either enumerators or individuals filling in their forms. For example, in the definition of 'rooms' in 1951 it was stated that only those rooms used for living, eating and sleeping should be included. In certain cases it seemed that unused rooms such as a spare bedroom had been omitted and in 1961 instructions made clear that such rooms should be added. Because there was still some confusion over the inclusion of kitchens or sculleries, in 1966 separate questions concerning these rooms were added and completed by the householder rather than the enumerator, as in previous censuses. In the 1966 tabulations 'rooms' generally included all kitchens rather than only those used for meals, though tables were provided giving the number of rooms per dwelling and household according to the 1961 definition as well as 1966.

A second example is provided by the extension of the definition of 'household' from 1961 onwards to include the exclusive use of at least one room. In 1951 some households were shown as sharing a single room.

(b) Omission to take care of certain categories which were therefore placed in one or other groups. For example, an omission to be explicit over the terms 'unemployed' and 'retired' in 1951 was rectified in 1961 when each was related to the week preceding the Census.

(c) Incorrect information given by some householders or individuals because the instructions given were unacceptable to them. For example, in 1951, schoolchildren, students and members of the armed forces living away from home were instructed to give their away address as their 'usual residence'. Many, however, were entered by their families as usually resident at the home address, and a change of definition was made in 1961 to accommodate this preference.

(d) Difficulty in using the definition provided. For example, in 1951 the registration of hospital inpatients as resident or not

depended on an assessment by the hospital authorities as to whether their discharge would be in less or more than six months. In 1961 in place of this, hospitals were grouped according to usual length of stay, length of stay since intake or type of care provided.

(e) The need for greater detail than has previously been provided either because of increasing interest in a particular area or a successful submission by workers in a particular area, or the realisation that earlier definitions obscured genuine differences. The great majority of changes between censuses are in this category. Examples are: the extension to questions concerning fertility made in 1961, and the identification of private quarters in institutions such as hotels or hospitals as separate dwellings, even though sharing access.

In Table 3, Census topics which have changed in definition in one or more of the postwar Censuses are tabulated with a description of the particular changes made. The greatest number occur between 1951 and 1961, no doubt a reflection of a new approach towards the Census by the GRO[3] in a period of greatly increased control by central and local government which led to a reassessment of all aspects of census information. The definitions provided in this table have been abbreviated, the purpose of the table being to indicate the nature of changes rather than to serve as a reference for the exact definition of terms, for which the explanatory notes of the subject volumes of the Censuses should be used.

The Reliability of Census Data

In chapter 1 the reliability of Census population data was considered largely in relation to the method of enumeration. Some mention was made of the post-enumeration checks made by the Registrar General but as far as the population count is concerned, these are of rather less importance than the comparison made with the annual estimates. For Census topics other than population, however, such checks are essential, particularly where data have been collected on a sample basis. Here errors of selection or

TABLE 3
Changes of definition in the Postwar Censuses

Subject	1951	1961	1966	1971*
Private household	One or more persons living and taking main meals together	As 1951, but with the exclusive use of at least one room	As 1961	As 1961
Non-private household	At least 10 persons, the number of boarders, etc., exceeding the number of persons in the family of the head of household	At least 5 boarders, etc., plus the family of the head of of household	As 1961	
Usual residence of boarding schoolchildren students, members of the armed forces	School, college, barracks, lodgings, etc.,	Home address or married quarters	As 1961	As 1961
Institution: boarding houses, hotels, etc.	A dwelling with 10 or more rooms occupied by 10 or more persons, whether advertised outside as a boarding house, hotel, etc., or not	Identified by external assessment, seasonal boarding houses, etc., identified by local authority in larger resorts. Occupation not a necessary criterion	As 1961	As 1961
Usual residence of inmates of institutions	Institution is the usual residence where inmates or patients are not expected to be discharged sooner than 6 months	Determined according to type of institution (i) Institution of normally long stay, e.g. homes for blind (ii) Home if normally short stay, e.g. general hospitals (iii) Institution in, e.g., psychiatric hospitals, prisons if residence has already lasted 6 months	As 1961	

TABLE 3 *(cont'd)*

Subject	1951	1961	1966	1971
Dwellings within a building	Accommodation with independent access to the street, or common landing or staircase with public access	As 1951, but with more than one living room in addition to kitchen and bathroom: except for 1 room flat with sep. kitchenette or sep. bathroom and W.C.	As 1961, but specified that access must be from one room only	As 1966
Dwellings in institutions	Not identified as such	Private quarters counted as dwellings if occupied by a private household	As 1961	As 1961
Room	Used for living eating and sleeping; no specific mention of rooms temporarily not in use; kitchens not used for meals and sculleries excluded	As 1951 but specific inclusion of rooms such as spare bedrooms etc. not in continual use	As 1961 but all kitchens defined as rooms whether used for meals or not and scullery if used for cooking	As 1961 but specific exclusion of kitchens less than 6ft wide and sculleries not used for cooking
Piped cold water	Must be reached without leaving shelter of building or an attached covered structure	As 1951 but without mention of attached covered structure	As 1961	As 1961
WC	Any location	Must be within the building or attached to it but entrance could be inside or outside	Within building but location of entrance specified	Not specifically within building, location of entrance specified
Fixed bath	Not specified	'Fixed' if connected to a wastepipe leading outside	As 1961 plus connection to a water supply	As 1966

TABLE 3 *(cont'd)*

Subject	1951	1961	1966	1971
Occupation	'Usual' employment by which the living is earned	Employment in the week before Census day	As 1961	'Main' employment in week before Census day
Out of employment, retired	No time reference	Referred to the week before Census day	As 1961 plus other periods (see Table 2)	As 1961
Part time	Less than 30 hours a week where at least 30 hours is usually worked	Less than the normal hours in the employment	As 1961	
Social class‡	Based on occupation only	Based on occupation and employment status	As 1961	As 1961
Socio-economic classification‡	13 group classification	17 group classification		
Industrial classification‡	Based on 1948 Standard Industrial Classification	Based on 1958 Standard Industrial Classification	As 1961	
Occupational classification‡	Based on 1951 Classification of Occupations	Based on International Standard Classification of Occupations 1958	Comparable with 1961, some division into sub-groups	Comparable with 1961, more detail in prof. and technical occupations

* Entries for 1971 are not always complete because information is not available at the time of publication.

‡ See chapter 3, pp. 88–96.

definition may lead to seriously biased information, while scarcely affecting the total population count.

1951

In 1951, comparative use was made of birth and death registrations and marriage entries to assess the reliability of data relating to age, marital status, duration of marriage, occupation and, for married women, year of last marriage, and number of children.[4] Generally the magnitude of discrepancies revealed in this way was low. It was found that there was a tendency, mainly by men, to anticipate their age at the next birthday. Women were also liable to inaccuracy in this respect, but about the same proportion tended to under-estimate their age, though mostly by only one year and rarely more than two. Again, proportionately few discrepancies appeared in the occupational returns and it seemed likely that the description provided at the census was usually more accurate than that at death registration where these differed.

After the 1951 Census, a small sample survey of households not sharing dwellings which had been recorded as without a w.c. was conducted. A relatively high proportion of errors was discovered here, largely because 'outside' w.c.s had been ignored, but the General Report makes the comment that although 'there may have been some appreciable overstatement of the lack of availability of w.c.s . . . [the data] do not exaggerate the estimation of obsolescence of housing accommodation'.[5] A similar survey to check statements concerning the availability of piped water disclosed some overstatement of those sharing or lacking this amenity.

Analysis of the differences between 1 per cent sample and non-sample figures completely vindicated the sampling procedure followed. Sample selection in 1951 was made by the GRO from census schedules—a very different procedure from that followed in 1961 and 1966. It is perhaps unfortunate that the success achieved was apparently not associated more closely with the method of selection used, until 1971.

1961

In 1961 the checks on data devised were considerably more elaborate than in 1951. In part this was because a substantial proportion of the questions were asked on a sample basis. These checks took three forms, the first two concerned with the coverage and quality of all Census topics, and the third with the validity of the sample:

1. A repetition of the comparisons with birth, death and marriage registrations made in 1951.

2. A post-enumeration survey carried out one month after the Census by enumerators who visited 2,500 plots throughout England and Wales, each plot containing about 20 households. No such survey was held in Scotland. Those findings which apply to the count of population have been discussed in the previous chapter (p. 26).

3. A comparison of 100 per cent and 10 per cent data at enumeration district and national level.

Coverage and quality checks: (i) Registration records. The sample for which birth, death and marriage registration records were examined was the same as that selected for and providing satisfactory returns in the post-enumeration survey, so giving additional comparisons with survey responses. In the great majority of cases, age declared at the Census was correct to the nearest completed year and most discrepancies were very minor. As in 1951, overstatement was more prevalent than understatement, and the latter was largely again a female characteristic. Children's ages were generally the most accurately stated.

Death registrations again revealed few age discrepancies, though agreement tended to be less good at higher years, particularly above the age of seventy-five. This appeared often to be associated with residence in an institution at death, when information for the death certificate was provided by the staff.

Death registrations were also used to check the accuracy of statements regarding marital status, and suggested some overstatement of married people. The majority of these discrepancies again occurred at higher ages and again were often associated with institutional residence. In other cases, however, it seemed likely that some older people had termed themselves married in spite of the death of their spouse.

41

Marriage registrations were used only to check statements of duration of marriage and showed agreement to within a year in 95 per cent of cases.

(ii) The post-enumeration survey. Generally, the post-enumeration survey gave more detailed results concerning a greater number of topics, but its success was limited by some defects in its organisation. This was the first time that such a survey designed as 'a census in miniature' had been conducted by the GRO, covering the whole of England and Wales. The complete sample of 2,500 plots containing about twenty households each was used to provide a coverage check on completeness of enumeration, while a sub-sample of about three households in each plot including two from the 10 per cent sample, was used for a 'quality check' in which detailed questions covering the Census topics indicated the quality of the information previously provided.

The limitations of the post-enumeration survey lay in the use of Census enumerators as interviewers, a decision made because it was considered that the survey would be more acceptable if conducted within a few weeks of the Census itself and under these circumstances the only practicable arrangement. Care was taken that no enumerator checked his original area, and Census Officers were asked to select the best of their enumerators available. Nevertheless, instruction was as limited as it had been for the Census, consisting of a short verbal briefing and written instructions. Generally speaking the coverage check gave satisfactory results but quality checks for certain questions, such as those concerning household arrangements, were often unsatisfactory.

The results of the coverage check, which largely concern the count of population have already been described in chapter 1. One part of this check intended, the identification of dwellings within the survey plots, was unfortunately omitted. That there had been some difficulty here became plain during the preparation of the sampling frame for the 1966 Census.

Inaccuracies revealed by the post-enumeration survey are summarised in Table 4. Exact figures are not given of the extent of under or over estimation in this table and for this reference should be made to the 1961 *General Report*, Part II, Statistical Assessment. The aim has been to indicate those topics in which discrepancies have been found, with a broad description of their nature. Data examined and found to be reliable relate to:

Birthplace

Nationality

Occupation, other than a tendency to use unspecific categories and inadequately described groups.

Industry

Household and family composition on a 100 per cent basis.

(iii) Sample validity test: (a) At enumeration district level the total number of persons, private households and persons in private households enumerated at 10 per cent and 90 per cent levels were compared. Where differences were found to be significantly more or less than one—tenth of the total count, the enumeration record book for the district concerned was examined. In the first instance, where the 10 per cent total was too low, it was found that some 10 per cent schedules had not been collected, usually because the household with which they had been left had moved away. This tended to occur in areas of high mobility such as lodging-house areas. In the second situation, where the differences were too small, schedules had been added, perhaps because in a recent move a schedule had been brought from another area or because unsorted spare schedules had been used.

(b) At national level comparisons were made between the full count and 10 per cent sample count of total population, population in non-private households, sex, age, marital status, private households by persons, rooms and tenure, birthplace and nationality. It was at this stage that the bias in the sample emerged, when it was found that there had been under-representation of those occupying one room and overrepresentation of those occupying many rooms. This clearly affected many associated characteristics. For example, old people, single males aged over twenty-five years, the

TABLE 4

The results of post-enumeration checks on the 1961 Census summarised from the 1961 General Report

Note: This table relates to variables other than population, which has been examined in chapter 1, and includes only those where some inaccuracy was indicated.

Topic	Groups concerned	Nature of inaccuracy
Usual residence	1. IN 90% ENUMERATION* School children Students Members of the armed forces Persons living at a different address at the weekend from the week	Some duplication leading to overstatement
Age	Age digit ending in 1, 3, 7	Avoidance of these endings, usually by ±1. Endings 0, 5, 8 favoured
	Middle-aged males Middle-aged and elderly females	Tendency to understatement, usually by not more than 2 years
Marital condition	Divorced	Tendency to understatement, especially in men, greatest in older age groups
	Women aged 25–39 years described as widowed	Tendency to overstatement, probably as substitution for single and divorced
	Men aged 65–74 years described as married	Tendency to overstatement, probably as substitution for widowed
Duration of marriage	All	Slight understatement generally by 1 year or less
Number of children	Childless women	Slight overstatement
Migration	Residents of less than 5 years' duration	Tendency to understatement, generally by rounding up Most errors within 1 year
	Residents of 1 year's duration	Understatement greatest here
Terminal education age	Education terminated at 14 years	Overstated
	Education terminated at 17–19 years	Slight understatement probable

* excluding those in 10% sample.

TABLE *(cont'd)*

Topic	Groups concerned	Nature of inaccuracy
Economic status	Out of employment	Some confusion between 'sick' and 'other'
	'Other persons economically inactive'	Overstated by including some retired and employees
	Apprentices	Overstated by including some 'other employees' and slight understatement leaving small net balance
	Part-time workers	Overstated by including some full-time workers, and understated by including some retired: leaving near balance
	Women, mainly married	Some economically active in 'housewives' category and vice versa resulting in net understatement of economic active
	Non-married women	Some housewives in 'retired' category
Social class	Social Class V, men and women (unskilled)	Some overstatement by including SC IV and a few SC III men
	Social Class IV, men and women (semi-skilled)	As above, partly balanced by including some SC V and a few SC III
Socio-economic group	Group 10, men and women (semi-skilled)	See SC IV above—inclusion of 9 and 11
Cold water tap	Sole users	Overstated by including persons sharing and without use
Hot water tap	Sole users	Understated
	No use	Overstated
Fixed bath	Sharing households	Some understatement where household shares in the same building or dwelling by inclusion in sole use
WC	Sole users	Overstated by including those with sole use of WC not attached to building
	No use	Understated as above

TABLE *(cont'd)*

Topic	Groups concerned	Nature of inaccuracy
Tenure	Persons holding accommodation by virtue of employment	Tendency to overstatement by inclusion of: 1. those renting with farm or business premises 2. those not needing to vacate premises at termination of employment
	Persons renting funished accommodation	Overstated by including those renting unfurnished
	Persons renting unfurnished accommodation	Understated by including those in all other groups
	Persons renting from Council	Overstated
Rooms	All households	Overstatement due mainly to the inclusion of rooms not used for eating, balanced by some understatement of kitchens used for eating. Gross overstatement higher in CB's than rural districts
	Households occupying 5 or less rooms	Slight understatement
	Household occupying more than 5 rooms	Overstatement

2. IN 10% ENUMERATION

Topic	Groups concerned	Nature of inaccuracy
Household composition	One person households	Understated through bias in sample
	Households with seven or more persons	Understated through bias in sample
Sex, age and marital status	Single males aged 25 years and over	Understated
	Persons aged 65 years and over	Understated
	Married persons aged 30-70 years	Overstated
	Persons aged 5–20 years	Overstated
	Widowed and divorced	Understated
Hotels and boarding houses	Managers, staff and their relatives	Overstated
	Guests	Understatement, especially of resident guests

TABLE *(cont'd)*

Topic	Groups concerned	Nature of inaccuracy
Other non-private households	Hospitals, homes, etc. Homes for disabled	Small overstatement of staff Small understatement of staff and overstatement of patients
Private households/ persons/ rooms	Households in dwellings occupying many rooms Households sharing a dwelling	Overstatement, increasing with number of rooms occupied Understatement of households, slight understatement of people within them
Use of stove and sink	Sharing households without exclusive use	Understatement of all sizes of households, greatest for smallest and largest
Tenure	Owner occupying households Persons renting with farm or business Persons renting furnished accommodation Persons renting unfurnished accommodation Persons renting by virtue of employment	Overstated Overstated Understated Some understatement Some understatement In all groups, gradient associated with number of rooms (see above) is superimposed
Birthplace and nationality	Citizens of Commonwealth countries and Irish citizens Men born in Nigeria and Cyprus Men born in Pakistan Persons born in the West Indies Aliens	Understated rather more for men than women Slightly understated Strongly understated Understated Understatement, especially of those of Italian and Spanish nationality

NOTE: This is a summary; more detail will be found in the Census 1961, *General Report.*

widowed and divorced, those renting accommodation, migrants and aliens are generally underrepresented, while married people between the ages of thirty and seventy years, and owner occupiers are overrepresented. The inaccuracies noted in Table 4 include those due to this bias. Bias was particularly strong in rural districts. There seems little doubt that there had been some substitution of 10 per cent schedules by enumerators in order to avoid difficulties such as might occur among the elderly or recently arrived immigrant from abroad.

In order to reduce the impact of the bias as far as practicable, bias factors have been provided by the GRO for tables based on the 10 per cent sample, and these are published at the front of each of the respective subject volumes. However, it would be an impossible task to provide them at every level for which data are available and they are therefore given only for large areas and the more important subgroups. The extent of the bias at lower levels, particularly within enumeration districts is an unknown factor and the possibility of distortion must always be kept in mind when using these figures, which are usually best considered as qualitative indicators rather than as exact quantitative measures.

1966

Checks on age distribution in this sample Census have been described in chapter 1 with the suggestion that under-enumeration in certain age groups was a result of some loss of members of households containing more than six persons.

In addition to the use of registration certificates and school records for comparative purposes a number of other post-enumeration checks have been briefly described in the introduction to the later Census reports. These consist of a number of checks on omissions, and a check on the sampling procedure. Four types of checks on omission are described:

1. In each Census district a small plot was randomly selected containing about fifteen dwellings. These were listed and compared with the 1966 sampling frame used. Deficiencies of rather less than 1 per cent were due to omissions in the 1961

list of addresses because they were vacant, not in residential use or under repair then.

2. An extended list of new hereditaments was obtained from the rating lists and a brief questionnaire sent to all householders in property occupied in April 1966. A 75 per cent response rate was obtained and indicated an omission of approximately 9,000 dwellings from the Census sampling frame.

3. A 10 per cent sample of all dwellings reported vacant, derelict or with households absent on Census night was visited and a proportion representing approximately 0·15 per cent of the population were found to have been occupied then.

4. A sample of 5,000 households enumerated in the Census was selected for a quality check conducted by the Government Social Survey.* Results suggested that between 0·11 and 0·29 per cent of the population had been omitted from the Census.

A check on sampling procedure was also made by comparing 1961 full Census data with 1966 at the same addresses. This provided no evidence for bias in the sampling procedure.

A full analysis of the 1966 Census results must await publication of the *General Report,* but the basic underenumeration is clear. It has been estimated that altogether about 57,000 people who should have been included in the sample, were not, and it appears likely that the omissions are not evenly spread throughout the country— the GRO states that in Greater London, for example, they are almost certainly higher than the average overall and clearly any area in which large-scale private building had taken place not long before Census day was open to a disproportionate risk. How far these losses will affect Census data other than population is difficult to estimate.

1971

The Registrar General's 1971 Annual Estimates take into account the Preliminary Census counts and it is made clear that under-enumeration has resulted from the large number of forms to be

---

* Now published in *A Quality Check on the 1966 ten per cent Sample Census of England and Wales* by P. Gray and F. Gee, H.M.S.O., 1972.

returned direct to the Office of Population Censuses, many still requiring completion. An estimated addition of 155,000 has been made to the population count to allow for these omissions. Preliminary results of the Advance Analysis were used to provide mid-1971 estimates by sex and age group[6] and again the need to adjust for underenumeration is noted.

No further information concerning the reliability of this Census is available at the time of writing.

SAMPLE CENSUSES: SAMPLING ERROR

Data from the 1 per cent sample taken in 1951 and the 10 per cent samples of 1961, 1966 and 1971 are subject to sampling error, error which arises inevitably when information is collected from less than every member of the population. Where a sample has been selected by random methods it is possible to provide for each attribute or variable for which data are available, a range of values within which there is a known probability that the population value lies. The magnitude of this range will depend largely on how high a probability of success in containing the population within its limits is required: the higher the probability, the wider the range. In addition the number of units in the sample influences its size: the larger the sample, the smaller the range.

The range of values set by confidence limits on either side of the value obtained from the sample is given by a statistic known as the standard error. This is used in combination with a factor, whose size is determined by the probability selected—for example, if a 95 per cent probability is required the factor will be 1·96; 95 per cent confidence limits attached to a proportion would then be

$$p \pm 1.96 \times \sqrt{\frac{p(1-p)}{n}}$$

where p is the proportion,

n is the number of units in the sample

and the Standard Error of p is $\sqrt{\dfrac{p(1-p)}{n}}$

Most Census data are provided in the form of counts, and in the 1966 Notes to the subject volumes, the GRO suggests that satisfactory values for the standard errors of these totals is given by their square roots. (In 1961 it was suggested that these should be multiplied by $\sqrt{0.9}$ to allow for the 10 per cent basis of the sample and non-replacement.) When such a standard error is multiplied by 1.96, the confidence limits so obtained, attached to the original value provide a range within which there is a 95 per cent probability that the population value lies.

An example may make this clearer. On Census Day 1966, twenty-five persons out of the 10 per cent sample of 9,983 enumerated in Wallasey CB were born in the Isle of Man or Channel Islands. Therefore in the *total* population of Wallasey CB on Census Day 1966, there is a 95 per cent probability that $10 \left[25 \pm 1.96 \times \sqrt{25} \right]$ persons were born in these areas, that is, between 150 and 350. The factor 10 raises the 10 per cent estimate to the total figure expected. Figure 1 enables the Standard error of Census totals to be read off graphically.

Where percentages or rates are published, the standard error appropriate to a proportion should be used after suitable conversion.* However, as confidence limits for these data are usually only of interest when they reach such a high level as to suggest that great caution is needed in using the figure, in 1961 the GRO indicated two levels in their published tables of proportions or rates. Where the standard error is between 10 and 25 per cent of the proportion or rate to which it applies, an asterisk – * – is used, and where it is above 25 per cent, the symbol used is ‡. The latter may also appear by zero entries as an indication that there may be a non-zero value in the population from which the sample is taken. Only the second level was indicated in 1966.

The two formulae for the standard error given above are applicable to a simple random sample with replacement and are not entirely suitable for Census data for the following reasons:

1. The 1961 and 1966 Sample Censuses were not randomly

---

* i.e. A percentage must be divided by 100, etc.

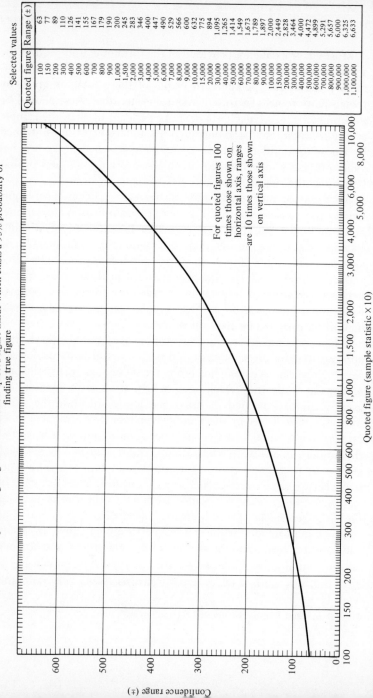

Fig 1. 10% Sample Census

Graph showing range above and below quoted figure inside which exists a 95% probability of finding true figure

For quoted figures 100 times those shown on horizontal axis, ranges are 10 times those shown on vertical axis

Quoted figure (sample statistic × 10)

Confidence range (±)

Selected values

Quoted figure	Range (±)
100	63
150	77
200	89
300	110
400	126
500	141
600	155
700	167
800	179
900	190
1,000	200
1,500	245
2,000	283
3,000	346
4,000	400
5,000	447
6,000	490
7,000	529
8,000	566
9,000	600
10,000	632
15,000	775
20,000	894
30,000	1,095
40,000	1,265
50,000	1,414
60,000	1,549
70,000	1,673
80,000	1,789
90,000	1,897
100,000	2,000
150,000	2,449
200,000	2,828
300,000	3,464
400,000	4,000
500,000	4,472
600,000	4,899
700,000	5,291
800,000	5,657
900,000	6,000
1,000,000	6,325
1,100,000	6,633

selected. Although planned to be so, bias occurred in both. This does not appear to be true of the 1951 sample.

2. The samples were stratified by enumeration districts, that is each district was independent for selection purposes.

3. The samples were based on households and not individuals except in the case of non-private households and were therefore cluster samples.

4. There was no replacement of selected households so as to be available for re-selection.

It is not possible to take account of the first factor as far as sampling error is concerned. The errors arising from bias may well far exceed the sampling error in many situations, but without evidence it is only possible to bear this in mind when using the figures.

The modification to the standard error required where a stratified or cluster sample is used will not be described here.[7] In general terms, the standard error of a stratified sample is smaller and that of a cluster sample usually larger than applies to a simple random sample. In the latter case the increase is related to the intra-class correlation which will be high where topics such as migration are concerned, when household members are likely to behave in the same way. A detailed examination of the inaccuracy involved in using a standard error applicable to a simple random sample for Census totals and proportions has been made by the GRO in relation to the 1961[8] sample. The 1951 sample is of a different character in that it formed the basis for provisional tabulations superseded by those from the full Census totals. Direct comparisons between sample and population could therefore be made, and the standard error for a simple random sample was found to apply well. Similar comparisons were possible to a limited extent in 1961 but not at all in 1966.

Tables are published in the 1961 *General Report* based on a comparison of the true and conventional variance and it seems likely that the range of ratios between the two would also apply in 1966. However, while in 1961 users were advised to multiply the standard error by a factor of $\sqrt{0.9}$ to allow for the 10 per cent basis of the sample and non-replacement, this was not done in 1966, so in effect increasing the size of the confidence limits.

CONFIDENTIALITY

The problem of retaining confidentiality becomes more evident when two or more Census data topics are combined. As a consequence, such tables may not always be provided in Census publications for small areas where the numbers likely to appear in some combinations will be low. In the Census of 1961, for example, most 3-way tables were provided in the subject volumes only for those urban areas where the population exceeded 50,000 even when the data had been collected on a 100 per cent basis, though Conurbation centres and New Towns were made exceptions because of their particular needs in relation to planning and redevelopment. In the 1966 Sample Census, the same level (50,000 and over) was used for nearly all the tables, though a few, including those in which data were simply listed, were provided for both urban and rural areas with populations exceeding 15,000. In 1961 and 1966 Ward Library population data were always available in full, though in fact a choice of levels was available which varied in price. In 1966, however, the Ward Library was extended to provide information at enumeration district level concerning journey to work and internal migration. In order to safeguard the anonymity of respondents, for very small numbers might well arise in some situations, the Registrar General required purchases of these data to submit to him any report based on its analysis before publication.

In 1971 the reduction in size of the enumeration district meant that in some rural areas very few households might occur. In order to preserve confidentiality in Ward Library tabulations the final figures in the cells of Population and Household tables have been modified by 'the addition of a quasi-random pattern of $+1$, -1 and 0. . . . The sum of the adjustments within a single enumeration district will tend towards zero as also will the adjustments to any individual cell when accumulated through a number of enumeration districts'.[9]

In addition only the number of persons by sex will be given for 'very small' enumeration districts and only the number of households where there are fewer than eight.

These measures, which apply only to the full Census information, for the 10 per cent sample selection is considered to be sufficiently concealing, indicate the serious concern with confidentiality in this Census.

COLLECTING AND PROCESSING THE POSTWAR CENSUS DATA

In many respects the Census of 1951 followed closely the style and organisation of prewar Censuses, but in those which followed there was a change of direction. In 1951 perhaps the most important consideration was a speedy provision of figures which would fill the twenty-year gap and give planners and government officers some statistical basis for their projects.

The 1951 Census was the last in this country processed by means of punched card machines. This type of machine was first used for the 1911 Census and so there was enough experience in the GRO in its use to make this part of the Census an efficient operation. After the provisional figures in the Preliminary Report the 1 per cent sample tables appeared only fifteen months after Census day. Later comparison showed a close correspondence between sample and full Census figures and it was concluded that 'there is no evidence . . . of any failure of the sample design'.[10]

In the 1961 Census punched card machines were superseded by a computer, shared with the Royal Army Pay Corps. There were high hopes at the start that the use of a computer would considerably reduce processing time, and that all programmes would be completed within four years. In the event, the last tables were produced in $5\frac{1}{2}$ years and it was only by extraordinary efforts on the part of the GRO that the delay was not longer. Inexperience in computer use, and problems related to its shared basis were largely to blame, followed by the additional work required when bias was discovered in the sample.

In 1966 the computer was no longer shared and production time was cut. Lessons had also been learned concerning the need for greater and more informal instruction at enumerator level. However, in concentrating on improvement here, perhaps less attention was given to other and as vital aspects of sampling procedure and a fully satisfactory enumeration was once more prevented, this time by an inadequate sampling frame. It would be an unkind stroke of fate if in 1971 the confounding factor arose through a combination of circumstances largely outside the control of the OPCS.

It has been pointed out that 1951–71 shows a progressively greater central control over the enumeration process and that this is linked with the increasing importance of sampling procedures. The 1951 Census was the first to introduce sampling, an innovation to be taken up in the next three Censuses, and one which will almost certainly appear in those to follow. At the time there was some criticism and a great deal of careful examination of the results. One detailed study by Silcock was particularly concerned with the variation in sampling error which occurs when a constant sampling fraction is used in areas differing widely in population size. He indicated three major defects in the 1951 sample which apply in some degree to those following:

1. The sampling procedure was not designed to prevent biased estimates. . . .

2. The general level of precision is too low for the tabulations to be of real service.

3. The precision varies too widely from one administrative area to another.[11]

It will be remembered that the 1951 1 per cent sample, like that in 1971, was intended to provide a preview of the results of the full Census, published during the next few years. In considering the use of a sample to replace a full Census, Silcock suggested two possibilities:

1. To reduce the 10-year interval between successive Censuses by interposing a sample survey,

2. To widen the scope of the full census by obtaining additional information from only a sample of householders.[12]

The second recommendation was put into effect in 1961 and the first in 1966, but in each case the potential advantages have been diminished by mistakes in procedure, leading to biased samples. These can largely be associated with the proportionately greater need for tight control when a sample is selected, without the administrative machinery capable of ensuring it. Such problems have forced changes upon the General Register Office, not least its recent merger with the Government Social Survey.

It cannot be denied that the adequacy of the Census, whether full or sample, depends on efficient enumeration and the importance of the enumerator has been recognised by those responsible for its organisation. In the 1951 *General Report* it was stated that 'the quality of the census results can be no higher than the quality of the answers supplied by the public allows, and the completeness and efficiency of the enumeration depends a great deal upon the efforts and personal qualities of the individual enumerators'.[13]

In any Census, however, even if on a 10 per cent basis, the dilemma is to recruit the thousands[14] of enumerators required of a sufficiently high standard when their recruitment is restricted to those free to carry out the time-consuming and at times exhausting work. The majority are local government officers and civil servants temporarily released from their duties, and most of the remainder are housewives and school teachers. Even in the more recent Censuses their training must necessarily be at some stages removed from that given by the specialist officers of the Census office.

If 1971 results should again reveal defects which are the direct responsibility of the enumerators, a fresh approach may be forced upon the OPCS. Now that it is more closely associated with the Government Social Survey, with its specialist skills and resources, it may be possible to consider the greater use of small samples at more frequent intervals conducted by well-trained and experienced interviewers examining particular topics in depth. The full census at five- or ten-yearly intervals could then concentrate on the count of population, households and dwellings which is still an administrative requirement.

The labour force

3

Labour force data have many aspects: the extent of employment and unemployment in general, their distribution by occupation and industry in particular. Information on these topics is available from a number of sources, not all derived from Census data as population estimates are. Only information concerned with manpower will be considered here, though most of the sources mentioned include a variety of industrial statistics.

The principal sources of manpower data, the sectors of the working population for which they are available, the dates when they have been published since the war and the level at which tabulations are provided are given in Tables 5a and b, which also indicate the breakdown of the total labour force made within these tabulations for each source. Additional information concerning the general character of the sources is given below.

CENSUS OF POPULATION

The Census of Population provides the most detailed information concerning the total labour force throughout the country (Table 2). Every Census of Population since the first in 1801 has included some information on type of employment, but each one has made changes in classification or interpretation, though these have become less comprehensive in recent years. Changes made in the postwar Censuses will be examined in pp. 88–96 of this chapter.

TABLE 5

Manpower statistics: Great Britain

(a) Censuses of population, distribution and production: postwar sources of manpower statistics

Census	Sector of the population	Year to which publication relates	Area covered (see key)	Level tabulated	Classified by:
Population	Economically active: enumeration applies to Census night (see Table 2 for additional specifications)	1951 1961 1966 1971	1–6 1–7 1–7 1–7,9	100% popn 10% popn 10% popn 10% popn	Sex, age, marital status, occupation, industry, etc. (see Table 2)
Distribution	Persons employed in the retail trade and closely related services: all those working in a specified week	1950 1957 1961 1966 1971	1–6* 1,2 1–6,8 1–3 1–6,8,9	Full sample Full sample Full	Sex, full-time/part-time, status (see text), kind of business, form of organisation, turnover
Production	Persons employed in manufacturing and allied industrial establishments: all those working in a specified week and the average employed in the year of the Census (1948 excluded)	1948 1951 1954 1958 1963 1968	1–3 1–3 1,2 1,2 1,2 1,2	Full detailed	Sex, age group§ status (see text), industry, size of establishment (number employed)

* Towns with a population of 2,500 or more
§ Under 18 years, 18 years and over

TABLE 5 *(cont'd)*

(b) Current manpower statistics regularly published in the Department of Employment Gazette

Sector of the working population	Month of estimate	Month of publication (usual)	Classified by :	Area covered (key, p. 62)
Total working population	Quarterly: June	February (provisional fig.)	⎫	1
	September	April	⎬ Sex	1
	December	July		1
	March	October	⎭	1
		Monthly	Time series of quarterly figures	1
Civilian labour force Total in civil employment	Quarterly (as above)	As above	Sex	1,3
		Monthly	Time series of quarterly figures	1
Employees in employment	Annual: June	February (as provisional fig.)	Sex and industry (MLH)‡	1
			Sex and age group‡	1,3
		March	Industry (MLH)	1,3
	Quarterly (as for working population)		Sex	1,3
	Monthly		Industry (Orders), time series of quarterly figures	1
			Time series of total figs.	1,3
Employees in employment in index of production industries (Orders II–XXI)	Monthly	2 months later	Sex and industry (MLH)	1
Total employees	Annual: June	February (as provisional fig.)	Sex and industry (MLH)	1
			Sex and age group	1,3
		March	Industry (MLH)	1,3
	June	September	Sex and age group (single years)	1
			Sex and 5-year age groups	1,3
			Sex, 10-year age groups and industry (Order)	1
	Quarterly (as for working population)		Sex	1,3

‡ Minimum list heading of the Standard Industrial Classification.

TABLE 5b *(cont'd)*

Sector of the working population	Month of estimate	Month of publication (usual)	Classified by :	Area covered (key, p. 62)
Employees in engineering and related industries (Order VII to XII)	Annual: May	March	Occupations within Industry (Order) by sex, age,§ full- or part-time, training	1
Women employees	Annual: June	September	10-year age groups and marital status	1
Married women employees	June	September	Industry (Order)	1
Registered unemployed	Monthly	Following month	Sex	1,3
			Age group§	1,3
			Duration	1,3
			Sex and age group§	10 (selected) and development areas
			Sex and industry (MLH)	1
Wholly unemployed	6 monthly: January	February	Sex, 5-year age groups and duration	1
	July	August	Sex, 3 age groups and duration	1,3
	Quarterly: December	February	} Occupation and sex	1
	March	May		1
	June	August		1
	September	December		1,3
	Monthly	Following month	as Registered unemployed Age group§ and duration	1
Temporarily stopped	Monthly	Following month	as Registered unemployed	
Unemployed coloured workers	Quarterly: February	April	} Sex, area of origin, age§	1,2,3
	May	July		
	August	October		
	November	January		

TABLE 5*b* (cont'd)

Sector of the working population	Month of estimate	Month of publication (usual)	Classified by :	Area covered (key below)
Local authority employees	Annual: June	November	Sex, department or service	1,2
Young persons entering employment	Annual total for year previous to publication	July	Sex, age: 15, 16, 17 years	1,3
			Sex, type of employment by age of entry	1,3
			Sex, Industry (Order), type of employment	1
Administrative, technical and clerical workers in the manufacturing industries	6 monthly: October April	January July	Sex and industry (Order)	1
Women in part-time employment in the manufacturing industries	Quarterly: December March June September	February June August December	Industry (Order)	1

Key to Areas covered:

1. Great Britain
2. Country
3. Region
4. County
5. Conurbation
6. Local authority areas
7. Wards, Parishes and enumeration districts
8. Shopping centres
9. Grid Square
10. Employment Exchange areas

CENSUS OF DISTRIBUTION

The Census of Distribution was first taken in Great Britain (excluding the Isle of Man and Channel Islands) in 1950 and was followed by Censuses in 1957, 1961, 1966 and 1971; in Northern Ireland the first was in 1965 and the second in 1971. Those in 1950, 1961 and 1971 were 'full' enquiries.

The function of the Census of Distribution is 'periodically to provide a detailed analysis of the structure of the retail trade',[1] that is nowadays, shops, stalls, credit traders and service trades such as hairdressers, boot and shoe repairers and the building trade.[2] Information is provided on postal returns and relates to either the calendar year or business year. Before 1968 the responsible body was the Board of Trade Census Office but in this year its organisation was taken over by the new Business Statistics Office, though still largely a concern of the Board of Trade, and its successor in 1970, the Department of Trade and Industry.

All Censuses of Distribution, sample or not, have included figures of 'persons engaged', although within this category the breakdown is minimal. The following subdivisions are made:

(a) Sex

(b) Full-time and part-time (1961, 1966 specified part-time workers as those normally not working more than thirty hours).

(c) Status:
    (i) Owners working in the business and relations not receiving a definite wage for their work in the business
    (ii) Paid employees given a definite wage, salary or commission.

These two categories have been used in all the Censuses though slight differences in terminology have occurred. The figures relate to a specified week in October except in 1950 when the last week of June was chosen.

Although basically including all retail organisations, there have been some changes over the years, largely the inclusion or exclusion of marginal type businesses and the specification of newly developed businesses. These have been related in part to changes in the Standard Industrial Classification.

The main variations are shown below.

Type of business	1950	1957	1961	1966
Agricultural suppliers	I	E	E	E
Dealers in coal	I	E	E	E
Builders merchants	I	E	E	E
Street pedlars, etc.	I*	I*	E	E
Vending machine operators	E	I	I	I
Laundries, laundrettes, etc.	E§	E	I	I
Repair work on consumer goods	E	E	I	I

(E = excluded, I = included.)

---

* But a low response rate, only 25 per cent in 1957.
§ Included in the Census of Production until 1953.

Two groups excluded in all Censuses may be noted: auction sales rooms (perhaps because of the practical aspect), and canteen workers, who are now considered more appropriately to belong to the manufacturing establishments in which the majority work. However, they were also excluded from the principal analyses of the full Censuses of Production until 1958, although in 1951 and 1954 their numbers with other ancillary workers were given separately.

Although the amount of information provided by businesses has sometimes depended on the size of the firm, all those included in the Census are asked for the number of persons engaged and the turnover (defined as total trading receipts) of the business for the year. Sample selection has varied to some extent from one Census to another, but in all of them every large organisation such as a co-operative society or multiple retailer has been included. Where samples have been selected, this has been on an area basis, the sampling fraction decreasing with population size except in areas of special interest.

Only in the full Censuses of 1950, 1961 and 1971 are the analyses published on a local authority basis, although data for towns included in the 1966 sample were available as special tabulations. 1950 data are provided for towns with populations of 2,500 or more, in 1961 for all towns, rural districts and shopping centres within towns. At the full Census of 1971, grid references were allocated to premises, promising even greater detail and some integration with Census of Population data for the same year.

Although as far as manpower data are concerned, there is a lack of detail in the Census of Distribution, it is the only source of information concerning the number employed in the retail trade according to the type of business and its turnover, and associated with the average wage and salary paid (Table 5a).

THE CENSUS OF PRODUCTION TO 1968

This Census was first taken in 1907, and then at close intervals until 1948. Between 1948 and 1968 it was carried out annually in Great Britain (excluding the Isle of Man and the Channel Islands) and from 1949 similarly in Northern Ireland, either on a sample or 'full' basis. A detailed account of all Censuses taken between 1907 and 1960 is given in *Guides to Official Sources,* no. 6.[3]

The Census of Production again relies on information provided in postal returns completed by establishments 'whose labour contributes to the sale value of goods'.[4] This includes both private and nationalised industries and also local and central government establishments within the Orders concerned.

A full detailed Census was taken in 1948, 1951, 1954, 1958, 1963 and 1968. It was only in these detailed Censuses that information on manpower was collected and until 1963 this provided the only source of information on employment in the manufacturing industries related to size of establishment (other than the simple dichotomy used in the Censuses of Population). The figure given by participating firms was the average number in their establishment during the year of the return and was estimated from the number of employees whose National Insurance cards were held in the last week of each calendar month. Until 1958 the number employed in a specified week was also provided. The following subdivisions were made:

(a) Sex

(b) Age: below 18 years, 18 years or over.

(c) Status:

(i) Working proprietors: self-employed and members of the family without a fixed wage or salary.

(ii) Employees:
Administrative, technical and clerical workers.
Operatives: all manual workers, separated in 1968 into:
Persons employed in transport work
Others.

Both part-time and full-time workers were included but were not distinguished.

Comparison between Census years must again take into account changes in the Standard Industrial Classification. Some changes from a manufacturing to a distributive or service classification affected the 1954 Census, while in 1958 changes to manufacturing included ancillary activities such as canteen workers, tree felling by saw millers, fish curing by the manufacturers of fish products. The majority of changes, however, have been due to greater detail in some groups where industries within certain sectors such as chemical and engineering, have developed. Such changes were most evident in the 1968 Census.

In the years in which a full Census was taken all firms included provided manpower data, but the amount of additional information varied according to the size and type of the firm. A detailed questionnaire including questions on capital expenditure, wages and salaries, transport payments, sales and work done, was sent to all firms concerned, with more than ten employees before 1958 and with twenty-five or more employees from 1958 onwards. These were termed 'larger firms'. 'Smaller firms' with fewer employees, other than those in the construction industry, provided only a statement of work done and the average number of persons employed, except where such firms formed a relatively large proportion of the particular employment and output they were concerned with. If so they were given a simplified version of the detailed questionnaire, as were the firms in construction.

The analyses all include information on wages and salaries, and in 1968 contributions to national insurance and private pension schemes were also incorporated. Full Censuses of Production are unique up to 1968 in relating employment within manufacturing industries to a range of employee size groups. Associated information and the areas for which it is provided are shown in Table 5a.

THE CENSUS OF PRODUCTION, 1970 SERIES

There was inevitably a considerable time lag between the collection of information for the Census of Production and its publication which substantially reduced the value of the data. Delay in sending in the returns was added to the need for exhaustive checks, careful classification and detailed analysis. Publication of the last of the 1963 Census of Production reports was in 1970: first reports of full Censuses usually show a three-year delay. The 1968 Census was the last of its series mainly for this reason.

The new series which began in 1970 is based on a central register of business establishments classified by size, location, industry and other significant characteristics. From this basis enquiries can be focused on particular areas of industry. The Register is currently still being compiled by the new Business Statistics Office, an interdepartmental servicing unit under the Director of the Central Statistical Office. Quarterly, annual and periodic enquiries will take over the functions of earlier Censuses of Production and extend their analyses.

The first new Census of Production was taken in 1970 in the mining, manufacturing and public service industries. As in the earlier series, all businesses with twenty-five or more employed were included and in addition some of particular importance with more than ten employed. Again statistics of manpower were obtained, in the four status groups identified in 1968. The newer,

more streamlined methods on a broader front enabled the preliminary results to be available within a year.

The annual enquiries will in future be largely produced by an
aggregation of quarterly enquiries covering different industries,
supplemented by a small amount of additional information. There
will also be less regular analyses of a more specialised type.[5] It is
estimated that an additional 15 per cent of businesses will be
involved.

DEPARTMENT OF EMPLOYMENT STATISTICAL SERIES TO 1973

The importance of manpower statistics is reflected in the regular
provision of figures by the Government Department concerned:
until 1968 the Ministry of Labour, from 1968 to the end of 1970
the Department of Employment and Productivity and since then
the Department of Employment. These figures are obtained mainly
from counts of insurance cards and from returns completed by
employers, and first appear in the Department's own publication,
now the *Employment Gazette*.

These data relate to the total population in work or seeking work,
but in some respects, such as area, in less detail than is given by
the Census of Population. In addition to counts within industries
and broad groups of occupations, information is given on labour
turnover, short time, overtime, salary and wage rates, normal hours
of work, hours lost through illness, holidays and strikes.

The detail in which information is obtained is largely dictated
by the method of its collection. The minimal detail, so far as
employment data are concerned, found in the Censuses of Distribution and Production is closely related to their dependence on
postal enquiries. The content of the returns used by the Department of Employment is similarly affected by their origin, and no
doubt changes in organisation due to arise in the near future will
effect equally fundamental changes in the data provided. An
account of the statistics published by the Ministry of Labour and
National Service up to 1958 which also describes how they were
obtained is given in *Guides to Official Sources* no. 1,[6] while a more

recent description of methods bringing the account up to date is available in the Introductory Notes in *British Labour Statistics Historical Abstract, 1886–1968*.[7]

To date, these statistics depend largely upon the two sources now examined: records of insurance contributions and information from certain firms and institutions.

Insurance contributions

Since 1948 every person in employment except a small group of self-employed is required to make insurance contributions if they are working for pay or profit or unpaid but under a contract of service. The exempted self-employed group consists of men aged seventy years or more, women aged sixty-five years or more and women below this age who are married and have opted out of the insurance scheme. In the great majority of cases, contributions are made in the form of stamps attached to insurance cards held for employees by their employers who buy the stamps, deducting that part of the cost met by the employee from his wage or salary. Cards need not be held by non-industrial civil servants or post office workers, and their contributions are recorded centrally. Although the administration of social security benefits is the responsibility of the Department of Health and Social Security, their records are used by the Department of Employment to obtain information concerning the labour force.

The reference number on each card is followed by a letter: A, B, C or D. Each card is valid for a period of twelve months and at the end of this period must be returned to the local office of the Department of Health and Social Security to be exchanged for a new one, on a date which depends on the suffix letter. The exchange takes place at the end of each quarter, 'A' cards in March, 'B' cards in June, 'C' cards in September, and 'D' cards in December. Losses through death or withdrawal from employment are believed to remain relatively constant and equally distributed, so that about a quarter of all cards are renewed each quarter, when a count is made by the Department of Health and Social Security, used since 1965 to provide quarterly estimates of total employment published by the Department of Employment. This includes all members of the working population and the count of cards received for exchange, whatever their suffix, is used, with estimates of those not holding cards. A June count of 'B' cards is the basis for a detailed industrial analysis, and because many cards are exchanged late or during the wrong period, all those received in the following three months are now taken into account for this analysis and an estimate is made of those still outstanding. In addition to these counts, samples of records held by the Department of Health and Social Security are used for special analyses. A 1 per cent sample is used for the annual mid-year analysis of employees by age, which appears in the September *Gazette*.

The insurance card which belongs to a person who becomes unemployed for any reason and is not going directly into new employment is left at the employment exchange where unemployment benefit is drawn, or at the Youth Employment Office for those less than eighteen years old. The card remains at the exchange or office until a new job has been obtained, and is also renewed at the appropriate time.

The exchange of cards will terminate in 1973 and after this time the annual Census of Employment introduced in 1971 will be the basis of all Department of Employment statistics (see p. 76).

Employers' returns

There are two forms of returns provided directly by employers
(a) A voluntary return (ED 205) giving a count of all insurance cards held by them at the beginning of June whatever their suffix. Most employers with five or more employees make these returns, estimated to cover about 87 per cent of all employees.
(b) Monthly returns, known as 'L' returns sent in by all firms in the manufacturing industry with more than 100 employees and a sample (about 25 per cent) of those with between 11 and 99 employees.

A sample of firms in distributive trades and some services such as catering and laundries also sends returns. Similar figures for persons employed in nationalised industries are supplied and for those in agriculture, building and contracting, and the civil service, for each of whom a Government Department is responsible. The monthly returns state the number employed currently and in the previous month, so providing a basis for estimates of change in the employment position over the month.

Sections of the population for whom estimates are made

The following sections of the working population are identified by the Department of Employment and estimates given throughout the year in the Department of Employment *Gazette* (see Table 5*b*):

(a) The working population, including:

Employers and self employed
Employees in employment (including those temporarily stopped)
The wholly unemployed
HM Forces: serving UK members of the armed forces and women's services including those on release leave

(b) Civilian labour force, including:

Employers and self employed
Employees in employment (including those temporarily stopped)
The wholly unemployed

(c) The total in civil employment including:

Employers and self employed
Employees in employment (including those temporarily stopped)

(d) The registered unemployed including:

The wholly unemployed
The temporarily stopped (otherwise included with employees in employment)

Comparisons between Department of Employment and Census totals of the working population, employees in employment, and the wholly unemployed are made on pp. 81–88 of this chapter.

Some changes in the methods of estimating the constituent groups have occurred over recent years, and the methods currently used are described below. A comprehensive account of the methods used previously is given by Devons.[8]

Employers and self employed

The number in this group is based on the most recent Census of Population as a significant proportion are without cards. Nowadays there is interpolation between Censuses, a count of a sample of cards belonging to the self-employed (Class 2 cards) being used to estimate the change.

The Census definition is a self-selected definition and may at times be inappropriate. The Department of Employment also point out that there may be some in this group who have second jobs as employees and if so they will appear in their estimates twice.

Employees and employees in employment

The group 'employees in employment' includes all those employees who are not wholly unemployed, who are on an employer's pay roll—that is including those temporarily absent because sick, on holiday and temporarily laid off. It is estimated from the difference between the total number of employees minus the total number of wholly unemployed.

For the majority of employees the national insurance 'B' suffix cards with belated 'A', 'C' and 'D' cards exchanged at the beginning of June and during the following three months form the basis for the annual June industrial analysis first published as a provisional figure in the February or March *Gazette*. The quarterly counts which follow are less detailed, and provide estimates published within a shorter period (Table 5*b*). A number of sections of employees need special attention:

(a) Civil servants: many do not hold cards and their records are kept centrally. In addition, since 1965 about 12,000 civil servants stationed outside the United Kingdom have been included.

(b) Post office workers: many again do not hold cards and the situation is the same as that for civil servants.

(c) Merchant seamen: many do not hold cards, and special arrangements are made in some cases for their contributions to be deducted centrally. The Department of Employment state that no reliable estimate of the number of merchant seamen is possible, and the figure used since 1965 is based on such cards as are exchanged plus employers' returns.

(d) Persons who have not yet entered employment, for example school leavers, immigrants, re-entrants to the working population such as married women. These are registered as wholly unemployed and only after 1965 were included in the estimate of total employees.

(e) Persons working for a few hours a week: their inclusion will depend on whether they hold an insurance card. Many, particularly married women in domestic work, do not. However, any person is included as a member of the working population if they hold a card with at least one stamp on it which is exchanged. This means that some irregular workers such as seasonal workers and students or pupils over fifteen years of age who work during the vacation will, if their card is exchanged, be counted in the total of employees.

The total of employees given by the Department of Employment therefore remains one of *insured* employees and differs from the Census total for this reason (see pp. 81–85).

Provisional figures relating to June are published in the *Gazette* the following February or March by sex and age groups (below eighteen years, eighteen years and over) within regions of Great Britain, and by sex and industry, at minimum list heading level of the Standard Industrial Classification, for Great Britain as a whole. In the following month a regional analysis is provided.

Corrections are made as further information becomes available. In the following month the figures are incorporated in the quarterly estimates of the civilian labour force and working population. All quarterly estimates are now based on the quarterly card counts.

Monthly estimates published in the *Gazette* are now given only for those industries used to calculate the Index of Production and are based on the June figures adjusted by means of the employers' monthly returns (the 'L' returns) which state the number of their employees, including those temporarily absent, at the beginning and the end of the month. The change so indicated is incorporated in the totals, given as an industrial breakdown at minimum list heading level.

The regional distribution of employees gives rise to some particular difficulties. The cards are returned to the office of the Department of Health and Social Security nearest to the firm or organisation responsible for them and the preliminary analysis by geographical (employment exchange) areas is made on this premiss. However, there are discrepancies—for example, large firms with branches in a number of areas may hold all their employees' cards at their head office and exchange them all within that office's area. Transfers to the appropriate area are made by the Department of Health and Social Security but not on a fully comprehensive basis and usually not until the final June estimates have been published.[9]

Information for this purpose is now given on the employers' voluntary returns, where more than twenty employees work in an area other than that in which the return is given. Establishments situated close to exchange boundaries also create difficulties.

The unemployed will also tend to use the exchange nearest to their home. From July 1968 in an attempt to overcome some of these discrepancies between area of residence and area of workplace, unemployment percentage rates have been based on a number of Employment Exchange areas within which a high proportion of residents both live and work. These 'travel-to-work' areas were revised in 1970 and are now used for an analysis of employees by sex and industry. Civil servants and seamen's cards are omitted from local exchange areas and may distort figures for certain districts. Though again some attempt at distribution is made, this can be taken only to the regional level.

A comparison of regional totals of 1966 Census and Department of Employment data has been made and is discussed on pp. 84, 85.

The wholly unemployed

The Department of Employment definition of this group is 'registered unemployed persons without jobs on the day of the count and available for work on the day'. This distinguishes them from the 'temporarily stopped' who are also registered unemployed, but who are regarded as having a job and shortly to resume work.

The total of wholly unemployed is obtained from cards lodged at employment exchanges and youth employment offices. Counts are made monthly on the second Monday, public holidays permitting. Unemployed who have not left their cards at the Exchange, and this is true for many married women who can receive benefits through their husband's insurance, will clearly be omitted from the tables.

Monthly figures are published in the *Gazette* broken down by sex, age, (below eighteen years, eighteen years and over) and duration in broad groups for regions within Great Britain and for Northern Ireland. They are also given by sex and age only for development areas and many employment exchange areas, a high proportion of whose residents work locally (see p. 74). There is also a monthly breakdown by industry, at minimum list heading level. An occupational analysis is made quarterly and a more detailed breakdown by age twice a year (Table 5*b*).

Estimated totals of a number of other special groups are provided by the Department of Employment in the *Gazette*. These include:

The disabled. The total number of men and women on the Disabled Persons register is given monthly, those suitable for employment registered as unemployed and those unsuitable for employment. Annually there is an analysis by sex, age groups (below eighteen years, eighteen years and over) and nature of disablement.

Women in part-time employment. The number of women in manufacturing industries working not more that 30 hours a week is published quarterly (Table 5b). This figure is obtained from quarterly employers' returns.

Administrative, technical and clerical workers. The number of administrative, technical and clerical employees in the manufacturing industry is published twice a year (Table 5b). This figure is again obtained from employers' returns.

ANNUAL CENSUS OF EMPLOYMENT

Proposals for earnings-related social security, to come into force in 1973, will result in an end to the national insurance card which was first introduced in 1912. As the present series of employment statistics, described in the previous section, largely relies on counts of these cards, new methods are required to provide this information.

An annual Census of Employment to be carried out by the Department of Employment has been agreed, and the first full Census was in 1970. The names and addresses of all PAYE schemes, held by the Inland Revenue, provide a complete sampling frame. Employers with only one or two employees will in future be asked to complete the census form once every three years.

From 1972 this Census will provide industrial analyses previously obtained from the annual card count, and from 1973 it will provide the basis for all analyses made by the Department of Employment. It will differ from the national insurance card in being based on jobs—many people have two jobs, none should have more than one card.

Enquiry into the occupations of employees in the manufacturing industries, by the Ministry of Labour, 1963–69

Between 1963 and 1969 an annual enquiry was conducted— initially by the Ministry of Labour and finally by the Department of Employment and Productivity—into occupations followed within the manufacturing industries. The resulting information differed from Census of Population data in classifying the industries by size of establishment, measured in number of employees, as does the Census of Production.

Fourteen industry groups within Orders III to XVI were included (1958 SIC); shipbuilding and shiprepairing were added in 1966. All establishments with 500 or more employees and a sample of establishments with 11 to 499 employees were sent questionnaires; the response was approximately 95 per cent of establishments, representing about 60 per cent of employees.

Four major occupational groups were identified, two of which were subdivided:

A. Administrative, technical and clerical workers, subdivided into six categories

B. Skilled workers

C. Production workers with experience and/or some training

D. Other employees, subdivided into

   (a) warehouse packers
   (b) road transport drivers
   (c) canteen staff
   (d) labourers
   (e) other workers.

Employees within these groups were classified by sex, age group (below eighteen years, eighteen years and over), full-time or part-time and apprentices or others undergoing training.

The results were used for a number of special tabulations published in the *Gazette*. The function of this enquiry is expected to be covered by the 1970 Census of Production series and the last enquiry was therefore made in 1969.

The analysis was continued, however, for engineering and related industries only (Orders VI to IX, 1958 SIC; VII to XII, 1968 SIC) from 1969, and provide an annual analysis in the *Gazette*.

Statistics of other Government Departments, nationalised industries and similar bodies

All Government Departments and nationalised industries publish reports at least annually, and where they have responsibility for a work force of any size some information concerning it is included. The amount of detail is variable, but usually includes some breakdown by area and status. The list below includes those bodies with a large number of employees.

Department of the Environment: *Housing Statistics*[10] (quarterly publication)

Housing labour force in *(a)* Public sector, new work
(b) Private sector, new work
(c) Public and private sectors, repair and maintenance.

Classified into: Contractors
Direct labour

Area: EC Planning Regions of GB (map provided)

Department of the Environment: *Monthly Bulletin of Construction Statistics*[10]

Operatives employed by contractors in:

$$\left.\begin{array}{l}\text{public sector}\\\text{private sector}\end{array}\right\} \text{on} \begin{array}{l}\text{housing}\\\text{industry}\\\text{non-industry}\end{array}$$

Operatives employed by local authorities on:

$$\left.\begin{array}{l}\text{housing}\\\text{non-housing}\end{array}\right\} \begin{array}{l}\text{by}\\\text{region}\end{array}$$

Registered unemployed operatives by craft: by region

Area: GB, regions where stated.

British Railways Board: *Annual Report*

$$\left.\begin{array}{l}\text{Salaried}\\\text{Wages}\end{array}\right\} \text{staff in } (a) \text{ railways}$$

       (b) rail workshops
       (c) ships
       (d) hovercraft
       (e) harbours
       (f) hotels and catering.

Number of employees at beginning and end of year.

Recruitment and wastage

Net transfers between sections.

Area: GB

Post Office: *Annual Report*

Staff by Function: *(a)* Administration, HQ and regional
               (b) Savings and remittance services
               (c) Postal field staff
               (d) Telecommunications field staff
               (e) National data processing service
               (f) Purchasing and supply services
               (g) Sub-postmasters and caretaker/operators.

Staff by Business: *(a)* Posts, including Giro, Savings,
                    Remittance services
               (b) Telecommunications
               (c) National Data Processing
               (d) Central HQ.

Area: GB

National Coal Board: *Annual Report*

Total manpower (time series):   Recruitment, juveniles and others
                              Wastage and net change

Wage earners on colliery books: Age distribution

Weekly paid industrial staff: Under officials
                              Underground and surface

Craftsmen: Weekly paid
                     Daily paid by type of craft

Total industrial workers by industry

Total non-industrial staff

Area: Coal Board areas and GB

The Electricity Council: *Annual Report*

Number of employees and percentage change: previous year
previous five years

Staff by status: Managerial and higher executive
Technical and scientific
Clerical, sales, etc.
Industrial
Trainees and apprentices

Employees on training schemes by occupation group

Area: Electricity Council, Area Boards, Central Electricity
Generating Board, GB

The Gas Council: *Annual Report* and Reports from Area Boards.

Total manpower (time series)

Manual grades:
  craftsmen and other

Staff grades:
  senior officers, office and other

production and products
distribution of gas
in conversion
general consumer service
accounts
administration and general
services

Labour turnover

Recruitment and wastage

Sickness and Accidents by sex and grade

Area: Gas Council and Area Boards (map provided) GB

British Airport Authority: *Annual Report*

Working population at airports: BAA employees
                                               Government employees
                                             Airline employees
                                             Concessionaires' employees
                                             Contractors' employees

Non-industrial ⎱
Industrial   ⎰ staff by function: administration
                                             engineering
                                           planning and commercial
                                                         management
                                           finance and accounts
                                           constabulary
                                           operations
                                           fire service
                                         traffic

Area: Airports and GB

British Steel Corporation: *Annual Report*

Total number of employees by divisions of industry:
               general steels, strip mills, etc.

Recruitment of graduates

Area: GB

COMPARISONS BETWEEN CENSUS OF POPULATION AND DEPARTMENT
OF EMPLOYMENT STATISTICS

Economically active and working population (Table 6)

The economically active population is the term used in the Census
of Population to describe all persons in employment in the week
before Census day and those not employed but intending to return
to work or obtain work. It includes those members of the enumerated population who are: *(a)* absent from work because sick, laid
off or on strike; *(b)* part-time workers; *(c)* members of the armed
forces, whether of the United Kingdom or not, if in this country
on Census night.

TABLE 6

The economically active population and the working population compared

Section of the population	Economically active population	Total working population (labour force)
	Term used in the Census of Population	Term used in Dept. of Employment statistics
Over school leaving age, below retiring age	Included if in employment the week preceding the Census unless currently in an educational establishment	Included if holding an insurance card if this is known to have been in recent use
Over retiring age	Included if in employment the week preceding the Census	As above
UK armed forces	Excluded if outside Great Britain on Census night	Included if outside or inside Great Britain
UK merchant seamen	As above	As above
Foreign and Commonwealth Armed Forces	Included if in Great Britain on Census night	All excluded
Foreign and Commonwealth merchant seamen	As above	As above
Persons intending to obtain work, not yet registered at an exchange (e.g. just left school)	May be included	Excluded
Unpaid workers, e.g. members of a family in their family business	Included	Excluded
Voluntary workers	May be included	Excluded
Employers and self employed	All included	Estimated if not holding insurance cards (certain age groups)
Part-time irregular workers (mainly women, e.g. in occasional domestic service, seasonal, agricultural work)	Included only if working in the week before Census day	Included only if holding insurance cards (many probably do not)
Employed with a firm based in Great Britain, abroad on Census night	Excluded	Included
Employed with a firm based outside Great Britain, in Great Britain on Census night	Included	Excluded

It does *not* include: *(a)* persons who only work occasionally or seasonally, if not working the week before Census day; *(b)* those currently attending an educational establishment full time.

'Working population' is the term used by the Department of Employment to describe all those in employment for pay or gain, available for work or registered as wholly unemployed at an employment exchange. It includes: *(a)* members of the United Kingdom Armed Forces, at home or abroad; *(b)* those currently attending an educational establishment if they are over school leaving age and are or have been in insured employment.

Although largely coinciding, therefore, the discrepancies between the two populations are sufficient to give totals which can differ significantly and comparisons have been made in order to identify the magnitude of those groups which are not common to both.

A comparison between the 1961 Census total and the (then) Ministry of Labour figure which allowed for the major discrepent groups resulted in the following table:[11]

Males and females	Total (thousands)
Census economically active population	23,816
Plus armed forces abroad	176
Plus British seamen at sea, *less* foreign seamen in British ports	63
Less foreign armed forces	29
Census based working population	24,026
Ministry of Labour working population	24,664
Difference	638

The difference was examined within sex, age and marital status groups and could largely be accounted for by the inclusion in the Ministry of Labour working population of young people attached to educational establishments but holding insurance cards and irregular workers with insurance cards—mainly married women, probably describing themselves as housewives on the Census form.

Persons in employment

Census statistics of persons in employment depend on the situation in the week before the Census. Although in 1966 additional criteria were used in order to allow closer comparisons with Ministry of Labour figures (see Table 2), this week has been used at least in part to define those persons in or out of employment in all postwar Censuses.

The Department of Employment statistics of persons in employment, included in its figures of the working population and civilian labour force and of which employees in employment form a part,[12] all depend upon the difference between those estimated as holding insurance cards in the current year, plus special groups such as self-employed and the armed forces (except in civilian totals), and those out of employment at the time the estimate is made. It therefore relies less on the situation in one particular week than does the Census, but because it is a derived total is liable to omissions which are not always readily observable or, if known, capable of being accurately assessed.

A comparison between the Department of Employment's estimate of employees in employment and 1966 Census of population totals was made in 1970[13] primarily to test the accuracy of the Department's regional totals. Information on certain groups of employees (mainly civil servants) normally not located more precisely than at regional level was obtained in 1968 and this was used to adjust to 1966 estimates.

The Department of Employment's estimates were over all nearly 300,000 higher than the Census, the proportionate difference being at its greatest in the Greater London area and other parts of the South East Region. In rural areas there was a tendency for the Census totals to exceed the Department's figures. The main reasons given for the discrepancies were:

(a) Students with national insurance cards included in Department estimates.

(b) Seasonal and irregular workers with cards, not working in the week before the Census.

(c) Some persons classified as out of employment (sick) included in Department estimates.

(d) Some persons classified as 'seeking work' in the Census who probably exchanged their cards and were included in the Department totals.

(e) Some persons claiming sickness benefit for more than a year probably described themselves as employees for the Census and are not included in Department totals.

(f) Some married women working for their husband might be included in the Census as employees, but excluded by the Department as self employed.

Differences at regional level could also be due to:

(a) Employees with no fixed place of work allocated to place of residence in the Census, and to either the area of card exchange or as 'unlocated' by the Department of Employment.

(b) Some employees wrongly located by the Department because the area of their work was not known.

(c) Difficulties in equating regional and exchange area boundaries with the local authority areas used for the Census. The administrative regions used by the Department of Employment are aggregates of employment exchange areas and do not coincide exactly with the Standard Regions. A table has been published in the 1966 *Ministry of Labour Gazette* indicating the discrepancies between the two at urban district, rural district or civil parish level.[14]

The unemployed

Some changes in the definition of the unemployed population have been made in each of the postwar Censuses in order to allow a closer comparison with Ministry of Labour and its successors' statistics, although in each one the week before the Census has been used as the period to which the work situation should relate at least in part.

The Census definitions of persons out of employment have been as follows:

1951: all those not at work during *the whole of the week* before the Census although seeking work, available for work, or sick.

1961: those not at work during *the whole of the week* before Census day because

either (a) sick—that is away the *whole* of the preceding week through sickness, but with employment to return to,

or (b) other—that is, seeking work or otherwise without employment available.

1966: those out of employment on the Monday before Census day,

    (a) in employment some time during the week, including seeking a job, waiting to take up a job after Census Day or sick, i.e. for *part* of the week,

or (b) out of employment during the week but in employment during the year, including seeking a job, waiting to take up a job after Census Day or sick, i.e. for the *whole* of the week,

or (c) not in employment at any time during the year, including the categories above.

Those in employment on the Monday before Census day but out of employment at any other time in the same week were classified as 'in employment'.

1971: those not at work during *the whole of the week* before Census day because

    (a) sick and without employment to return to though intending to seek work

    (b) seeking work or waiting to take up a job

    (c) other, not seeking work for some other reason.

In this Census, therefore, those sick for the whole week, but with employment to return to will be classified as 'in employment' and not distinguished in any way from those at work all that week.

The 'wholly unemployed' in Department of Employment returns, are those members of the working population with insurance cards who are registered as unemployed at an employment exchange. Counts are made on Mondays and relate to that day, so including a number who obtain work later in the week, and excluding those losing their job later in the week. The 'wholly unemployed' do not include those temporarily out of employment through sickness or injury; on strike, temporarily stopped or in casual work.

A comparison between 1951 Census population 'out of employment' and Ministry of Labour 'wholly unemployed' was not possible because of the inclusion of those sick but with work to return to in the Census figures. Separation in later Censuses has enabled comparisons to be made, and an analysis by age using 1961 Census data[15] gave the following results:

| Males and females | Age Group (thousands) | | | |
	15–19	20–24	25 and over	Total
Census 'out of employment, other'	59	53	268	380
Ministry of Labour registered wholly unemployed	24	34	242	300
Difference	35	19	26	80

The rather large differences were probably due to the exclusion from the 'wholly unemployed' of persons who fall into three groups:

1. Those who expect to take up employment in the near future but have not yet registered. These include school leavers, recent immigrants, members of the armed forces on leave pending discharge.

2. Those normally in part-time work who have not registered at an employment exchange— mainly married women. Many may not hold an insurance card. Some over retiring age may fall into this category.

3. Special groups registered separately by the Ministry of Labour, including severely disabled trainees at Government Training Centres and Industrial Rehabilitation Units.

These differences are likely to arise in all Censuses unless special steps are taken to distinguish these groups.

CLASSIFICATIONS

Classifications of occupation, industry and social class have been used for many years in Government statistical publications. Since the war they have been devised and revised by interdepartmental committees and with a few early exceptions have been based on proposed International Classifications, though differing in detail.

An examination of the current occupational classification leading to modifications and consequential changes in the social classifications derived from it, is made before each Census of Population and a revised *Classification of Occupations* volume is published in Census years or the preceding year. Industrial classifications since the war have been revised rather less frequently, at ten-year intervals. Change is inevitable as new branches of industry grow and old ones dwindle, but leads to great difficulty when comparisons are made over time. This is recognised by the Government departments concerned who nowadays publish or make available tables showing the correspondence between consecutive series for the more important classifications. Although often associated with the Census of Population, these classifications are used throughout the whole range of Government manpower statistics.

Occupational classification

Postwar *Classification of Occupations* volumes have been published in 1950, 1960, 1966 and 1970, by the General Register Office, that is before each Census of Population. Some revisions have been made in each edition, but the classifications used for the 1961, 1966 and 1971 Censuses are closely comparable.

Currently, four aspects of occupation are classified separately:

1. *The classification of occupations:* concerned with the type of work done and the conditions under which it is performed.
2. *Economic position and employment status:* the first concerned with employment potential, the second with the level of responsibility and position held within the work organisation.
3. *Social class:* the type of skill required for the work done.
4. *Socio-economic group:* groups within which there is an attempt to place together people of similar social, cultural and recreational standards using employment status and occupation as criteria.

The *Classification of Occupations* published in 1950 differed little from that used in the previous two Censuses: those of 1921 and 1931. Twenty-eight principal Orders were distinguished, the last containing those retired or not gainfully occupied and including students and those following occupations outside the UK.

In 1960 this last group was removed from the classification and placed within a separate category of 'economically inactive'. There was also considerable revision, including some reduction of detail within the principal Orders, the new classification being based on the 1958 International Standard Classification of Occupation, recommended by the International Labour Office. The General Register Office stated that their 1960 classification, with about 200 unit groups, was 'broadly comparable with the two digit level of the International Classification'.[16] In the two following classifications some divisions have been made within groups as a consequence of certain occupations increasing in importance in the intervening period, but at least at Order level, and largely within it, comparisons of occupational data classified under the three latest classifications may be made without modification. Between 1960 and 1966 expansion has occurred mainly within Order VII—Engineering and Allied Trades, and Order XXV—professional, technical workers and artists and few units have been dropped. Unit group numbers have also changed throughout so that they run consecutively rather than each Order starting at the next '10'.

Between 1966 and 1970 unit groups again run consecutively, the main changes being reduction in Orders II—Miners and Quarrymen, and XXII—Sales Workers, and expansion in Order XXV again. All revisions between 1960, 1966 and 1970 are set out in Appendix D of the *Classification of Occupations,* 1970.

On the other hand, the Introduction to the Occupation Tables from the 1961 Census states that a comparison between 1951 and 1961 occupational data is 'very difficult'. A subsample of 1961 Census data was coded by both classifications but it had been decided not to publish the results because of their uncertain validity.

In the Introduction to the 1970 *Classification* volume, some information is given concerning the criteria used to define a unit group.[17] These are:

1. Basically, that each group shares at least one common characteristic.
2. That the number of individuals in the group is likely to be large enough to be worth separate identification on a 10% basis.
3. That the group can be reasonably accurately identified from Census questions.
4. That there is sufficient interest in the group to justify separate identification.
5. That the group could not equally well be identified by a cross classification of occupation by employment status or industry.

A new occupational classification is being prepared for publication in late 1972, described by S. Tolson in the *Department of Employment Gazette,*[18] based on rather different principles from its predecessors. Classification will be by work content or job activity, and grouping will be based on the similarity of work done, rather than qualifications, status, skill or industry.

This classification resembles more closely than previous classifications the International Standard Classification of Occupations put forward by the ILO, and it is hoped that it will be used in all government statistics, including the Census of Population. It is suggested that it may be adopted by employers also.

The classification system is a detailed one, using eighteen major groups divided into minor groups which are given two-digit numbers. These are themselves subdivided into unit groups of occupation, identified by an additional digit after the two allocated to their minor group, and below this again, individual occupations are given two additional digits separated by a point from the preceding three.

The Classification will be published in three volumes and will be known by the code name CODOT.

Economic position and employment status were first introduced in the 1960 *Classification of Occupations*. Economic position separates those in employment or temporarily out of work from those outside the work situation. In 1966 a number of criteria were used to distinguish the unemployed (see p. 86) but economic activity was related, as in other Censuses, to the main gainful employment in the week before the Census was taken.

Again changes of detail occurred between Censuses, largely as clarifications. One major change was made in 1966 when family workers were classified as employees rather than as an independent group. Table 7 sets out the three classifications.

Size of establishment was used as a further refinement of the manager and self-employed categories 'to provide some measure of distinction between [those] with greater and less responsibility'. The distinction between 'large' and 'small' was made at the level of twenty-five employees, 'large' establishments employing this number or more.

A classification of civilian employed made in 1950 was based on a similar concept to employment status but was discontinued as an occupational classification. This was a division into 'salary earners' and 'wage earners'—terms which it was stated were not meant to be directly related to the basis of enumeration. Three subdivisions were made within each category, which largely separated non-manual from manual workers. As an industrial classification it was used until 1966.

Social class was first introduced into the 1921 Census of Population in the form of five basic groups still retained, and described as:

TABLE 7

Economic position and employment status classifications published in 1960, 1966 and 1970

Economic position	Employment status
1960:	
ECONOMICALLY ACTIVE	
Family workers	
Other occupied persons:	Self employed
	(a) with employees
	(b) without employees
	Employees
	Managers
	Foremen and supervisors
	(a) manual
	(b) non-manual
	Apprentices, articled clerks and
	formal trainees
Out of employment:	Professional employees
(a) sick (including the disabled)	Other employees
(b) other	
ECONOMICALLY INACTIVE	
Institution inmates	
Retired	
Students in educational establishments	
Other persons economically inactive	
1966, 1970:	
ECONOMICALLY ACTIVE	
Occupied persons	Self employed
	(a) with employees
	(b) without employees
	Employees
	Managers
	Foremen and supervisors
	(a) manual
	(b) non-manual
	Apprentices, articled clerks and
	formal trainees
	Family workers
	Other employees
Out of employment	
(a) temporarily sick	
(b) other	
ECONOMICALLY INACTIVE	
Retired	
Students in educational establishments	
1970 only: Permanently sick or disabled	
Other persons economically inactive (including the disabled in 1966)	

I.   Professional occupations
II. 'Intermediate' occupations, i.e. requiring lower qualifications or entailing less responsibility than I but more than III
III. Skilled occupations
IV. Semiskilled occupations
V.   Unskilled occupations.

The basis of the classification is said to be 'general standing within the community of the occupation concerned' and it is stated that although factors such as education and economic environment are closely associated, there is no direct relationship with the average level of renumeration of the particular occupation.[19]

Although the basic criteria have remained the same, changes have been made between the four postwar classifications in step with changes in the occupational structure. Those between 1950 and 1960 were particularly extensive and the more important are listed in the Introduction to the 1960 volume.[20] Three significant developments occurred in this year: first, the exclusion of members of the armed forces entirely from the classification, second the incorporation of employment status, so that the social classification assigned to a person depended upon this as well as their occupation, and third, the division of Social Classes II, III and IV into non-manual, manual and agricultural groups. This was of particular importance in Social Class III where the balance between non-manual and manual occupations is a great deal closer than in the other two classes and is of some sociological significance—this third development in fact transformed the social classification into one far more acceptable to research workers outside Government Departments than previously. No division was made in Social Class I or V, the first being classified as wholly non-manual, and the second as wholly manual. In 1970 the 'agricultural' category was dropped, all occupations previously so designated being placed in the 'manual' group.

Changes in classification between 1960, 1966 and 1970 are set out in Appendix D of the *Classification of Occupations*, 1970: very few alterations in social class are indicated.

Socio-economic classification was introduced in 1951 in order to provide more detail than did the five social classes, in a 'larger number of more sharply defined groups'. There were thirteen of these, combining status and skill. In 1960 the classification was completely revised and was based on recommendations put forward by the Statistical Commission and Economic Commission for Europe, resulting in sixteen groups. Definitions are given in the introductions to the Classification of Occupations 1960, 1966 and 1970. Few changes were made between these three years, and such as there are have been tabulated in Appendix D of the *Classification of Occupations, 1970*.

Because of the number of groups, this classification can only be of use where a large sample or population is involved. For this and for comparative reasons, a transformation from socio-economic to social classification may be required. This is usually made as follows:

Socio-economic group	Social class
3, 4	I
1, 2, 13	II
5, 6	III non-manual
8, 9, 12, 14	III manual
7, 10, 15	IV
11	V
16, 17	undefined

There are a number of discrepancies in the transfer, chiefly among the non-manual groups. Details of the two classifications in terms of common occupation units and employment status are given in Appendix B 2 of the 1970 *Classification of Occupations*, and a summary table relating them to each other in Appendix E of the same volume.

Industrial classification

Apart from the combined status and industrial classification of 1950 which has not appeared outside the earlier postwar Censuses, the Standard Industrial Classification (SIC) has been used for all

Government industrial statistics since 1948 when it was introduced in order 'to promote uniformity and comparability in official statistics of the UK'. In devising it the interdepartmental Committee of Government Departments took into account the International SIC of all economic activities recommended by the Statistical Commission of the United Nations. Two major revisions have been made to date in 1958 and 1968, though the general principles remain the same. These are given in the introduction to the classification volumes, and can be summarised as follows:

1. The classification is one of industries and all those employed in a 'unit' of industry are grouped together irrespective of the occupation they follow.
2. The 'unit' is the establishment—the whole of the premises at a particular address, whatever variety of activities are conducted there, unless records are available for separate departments engaged in different activities, when each is treated as a separate establishment.
3. The structure of industry and trade as it exists within the U.K. has been the basis of the classification.
4. Where two or more activities are conducted for which separate records are not available, the establishment is classified according to its major activity.

The major group into which an industry is placed is the Order—there are twenty-four of these in the first two SICs, twenty-seven in the last. At the next level is the Minimum List Heading (MLH) which in some cases may be further subdivided. Revisions to the SIC have been made to allow for changes in the industrial structure over time—these were particularly extensive between 1948 and 1958, with both additions and deletions of some MLHs, changes in the names of Orders and generally an increase of detail. In 1968 almost all changes involved additional MLHs including some upgrading from subdivisions.[21]

A comparison of the 1948 and 1958 classifications was published in the *General Explanatory Notes of the Industry Tables,* Part I, 1961 Census. This was descriptive, listing 1948 MLHs against

1958, and quantitative, reallocating the 1961 employed population to the 1948 SIC. In addition a similar reclassification of those employees in Great Britain appearing on employers' 'L' returns (see p. 70) was made by the Ministry of Labour using their September 1959 estimate.[22] Similarly when the 1968 SIC was used for the June 1969 annual estimates of employees and employees in employment they were also classified by the 1958 SIC and published in the following month.[23] A table is available from the Central Statistical Office (Great George Street, London SW1) containing a full comparison of the 1958 and 1968 SICs which will be published with the 1971 Census Industry tables.

Education 4

The increasing volume of publications, regular and special, since the last war, concerned with some aspect of education reflects the increasing importance placed on this subject by central and local government, this in turn perhaps reflecting and stimulating interest in the general population. In 1959 the Central Advisory Council for Education in their report *15–18*[1] spoke of 'most extraordinary gaps in our knowledge of what goes on in the schools and technical colleges we have today'. A great deal has been done since then to rectify this lack of information and some of the publications now available are described in this chapter. Education as a topic can be approached from a number of directions: its provision through various types of institution, the association between the standard attained and the occupation followed, the extent to which specialised requirements in the work situation are met, are perhaps the most obvious. Information on these and other aspects is supplied from a number of sources, but unlike the topics of preceding chapters, it is probable that research publications from independent and public bodies concerned with single investigations, equally with the regular provision of statistical data from official sources, supply that basic material which is in continual demand. In this chapter, therefore, there will be some mention of special reports, although it is only possible to list a small number of particular importance.

SOURCES OF REGULARLY PUBLISHED DATA

Data published at regular intervals during some part of the post-war years can be described as principally concerned with either:

1. *The institution*—including the organisation of all types of educational establishment, those for whom education is provided within them and those who provide it;

2. *The individual* within the labour force or available to enter it—the end product of the educational process.

Table 8 indicates current sources of information on general topics and the areas for which the data they provide are available. The sources themselves are described in more detail in the remainder of the chapter. The numbers in column 2 also appear in the text alongside the relevant sources (pp. 102–113).

TABLE 8

Current sources* of educational data: Pupils, teachers, students, school leavers, qualified employed

Subject	Publication (numbers correspond to those in text: pp. 102–113)	Area (key, p. 100)
1. PUPILS		
In all types of school including nursery	1	2,4,6
	7	3
	8	3
	15	0
	22	6
In Primary schools	14	1
At nursery schools	22	6
Above school leaving age	1	2,6
	15	0
Taking GCE courses	1	2,4
Taking GCE courses in science and technology	27	1,3
13 to 16-year-old, average ability or less	13	1
Taking dinners and free milk	5	6
	7	3
	8	3
	9	2
By country of origin	1	2,4,5
2. TEACHERS		
In all types of school including nursery	1	2,4
	4	2,4
	15	0
Not including nursery	26	8
In FE establishments	4	2
	12	1,2,3
	26	8

* Not including Censuses of Population (see Table 9).

TABLE 8 *(cont'd)*

Subject	Publication (numbers correspond to those in text : pp. 102–113)	Area (key, p. 100)
In colleges of education	4	2
	12	1,2,3
	15	0
	26	8
In universities	6	1,2,3
	12	0,1
	15	0
In universities teaching science and technology	27	1
Qualifications—school teachers (maintained and direct grant schools)	4	2
Qualifications—teachers in higher education	12	0,1,2,3
Country of origin	9	2
Serving abroad—school teachers	9	2
Service abroad—university teachers	12	1
3. STUDENTS		
At colleges of education	4	2
	12	1
	15	0
At colleges of education taking science and technology	27	2
At universities: undergraduates	6	1,2,3
	12	1
	15	0
At universities: postgraduates	6	1,2,3
	12	1
	15	0
In FE establishments	3	2,4
	12	1
	15	0
Qualifications at entrance	12	2,3
	21	0
Degrees awarded	6	1,2,3
	15	0
Degrees awarded in science and technology	27	1
Courses taken	6	1,2,3,7
	12	2
	15	0
1st degree achievement	21	0
Failing degree course	12	2
	19	7
1st employment	7	3
	8	3
	18	2

TABLE 8 *(cont'd)*

Subject	Publication *(numbers correspond to those in text : pp. 102–113)*	Area *(key below)*
1st employment of science and technology graduates	27	1
Present employment of FE students	3	2,4
All admissions to universities	20	0
Place of residence	12	2
	17	1,2,3,7
Parental occupation or social class	12	2
	21	0
Area of origin	6	0,1,2,3
	12	1,2
4. SCHOOL LEAVERS		
All	2	2
Factors affecting age	11	1
	12	2
Qualifications	2	2,4
	11	1
	12	2,3
1st employment	11	1
	25	1
Destination (all)	2	2
Destination (applicants to universities)	21	0
5. QUALIFIED EMPLOYED		
Qualifications obtained after leaving school	11	1
Apprenticeships	11	1
Qualified in science and technology	27	0,1,2
	28	1

Key to areas

0. UK
1. Great Britain
2. England and Wales
3. Country (within U.K.)
4. Region

5. Aggregates of local authorities
6. Local education authorities
7. University towns
8. Local authority area

Sources principally concerned with the institutional aspect are:

A. Publications of the Department of Education and its UK counterparts and predecessors. (In Scotland, the Scottish Education Department, in Northern Ireland, the Northern Ireland Ministry of Education. In England and Wales, until 1963 the Ministry of Education, from 1964, the Department of Education and Science.)
B. Publications of the University Grants Committee.
C. The Annual Report and Statistical Supplement published by the University Central Council for Admissions (UCCA).
D. Educational Statistics, published by the Institute of Municipal Treasurers and Accountants.
E. The Census of Population, Education Tables, 1951 and 1961.

Those principally concerned with the manpower aspect are:

F. The Census of Population, Qualifications and Manpower Tables, 1961, 1966, 1971.
G. Publications of the Department of Employment.
H. Publications of other Government Departments.

THE INSTITUTIONAL ASPECT

A. *Publications of the Department of Education [and Science], its UK counterparts and predecessors.*

Annual publications

The sequence of postwar publications providing comprehensive statistics on this aspect prepared by the U.K. Ministry or Department concerned is shown below:

	Period	Publication
England and Wales	to 1960	*Annual Report* of the Ministry of Education, Part 2
	1961–1965	*Statistics of Education,* 3 parts annually
	1966 onwards	*Statistics of Education,* 6 volumes annually

Scotland	to 1965	*Education in Scotland*
	1966 onwards	*Scottish Educational Statistics*
Northern Ireland	to 1965	*Education in Northern Ireland*
	1966 onwards	*Northern Ireland Education Statistics,* twice yearly

The general topics covered in all these volumes are very similar though analysed in greater detail in the later publications. Five of the six volumes of *Statistics of Education* are the responsibility of the Department of Education and now separately include information on subjects originally contained in the Ministry's single *Annual Report* and currently in the Scottish and Northern Ireland reports. The titles of the six are:

Volume 1. *Schools*
Volume 2. *School leavers, CSE and GCE*
Volume 3. *Further Education*
Volume 4. *Teachers*
Volume 5. *Finance and Awards*
Volume 6. *Universities*

The last is produced by the University Grants Committee and replaces their pre-1966 publication: *Returns from Universities and University Colleges in receipt of Exchequer Grants.* Data in each volume are obtained from different sources.

1. *Volume 1. Schools.* The information is obtained from returns completed by each school for the Department of Education, relating to January. These include a count of teachers and pupils in each type of school and the average size of class. Some regional analyses are made, including one which gives pupils' country of origin. At local education authority level, the proportion of pupils one and two years above school leaving age and the distribution of thirteen-year-olds between different types of school is given.

2. *Volume 2. School Leavers, CSE and GCE.* The information is obtained from questionnaires sent to all schools and institutions in the public sector, assisted schools and independent schools recognised as efficient. These ask for the number, age and sex of

all leavers, and for 10 per cent of them, their destination on leaving school, and the results of any GCE or CSE examinations taken. A high response rate is obtained, only about 1 per cent of schools not cooperating.

3. *Volume 3. Further Education.* Returns from further education establishments to the Department of Education are made in November and provide the information in this volume. Universities and colleges of education are not included. The number of students on different courses and the type of courses available are given, some on a regional basis.

4. *Volume 4. Teachers.* Returns from colleges of education to the Department of Education are the basis of information concerning students and teachers. The Department's service and salary records are used for statistics relating to working teachers and these therefore relate only to teachers in maintained and direct grant schools. Transfers and moves out and in are recorded as well as age, sex, and qualification which are classified by type of school and subjects taken. Only one regional analysis is made.

5. *Volume 5. Finance and Awards.* This volume includes a statement of all forms of expenditure for which the Department of Education is responsible and again therefore covers only maintained and direct grant schools. Grants paid through the UGC are included and also the numbers of pupils taking dinners and free milk. Some information is given for local education authorities.

6. *Volume 6. Universities.* Information supplied by the UGC includes the number of undergraduates and postgraduates by age, sex, qualification entered for, subject group and country of origin, university income and expenditure. Unlike volumes 1–5, its data relate to all UK universities.

Comparable reports from Scotland and Northern Ireland are:

7. *Scottish Educational Statistics.* This annual publication began in 1966 and contains largely the same information as that included in *Statistics of Education,* volumes 1–5, relating to Scottish schools. The 1970 volume contains the results of a survey on the first

employment or training of graduates who qualified in 1969 in Scottish universities. This was extracted from the annual enquiry made by the UGC (see p. 107).

8. *Northern Ireland Education Statistics.* Now a two-volume publication, the spring volume contains information relating to Northern Ireland schools, pupils, teachers, teacher training, scholarships and awards, milk and meals provided and projections of the school population to 1990. The autumn volume is concerned with finance, school leavers, the results of examinations and further education.

9. *Educational [and Science] in 19—.* This annual publication is the report of the Department of Education and Science to Parliament, on the activities of the Department during the preceding year. The title corresponds to that of the Ministry or Department. Until 1960 its second part contained Statistics of Education. Data now provided in the Statistics of Education are the number of overseas assistants teaching in England and Wales by country of origin, and the number of teachers from England and Wales serving in Europe by their destination. The number of new schools built and the size of grants paid to organisations for further education are also included. Its most useful inclusion for the research worker is probably a list of the Department's publications during the year.

Special reports

10. A *Special Series* of reports have been published by the Department of Education and Science since 1968. To date there are four of these:

SS1. *Survey of the Curriculum and Deployment of Teachers (Secondary Schools), 1965/66.* Part I: *Teachers,* HMSO, 1968

SS2. *Survey of In-Service Training for Teachers, 1967,* HMSO, 1970

SS3. *Survey of Earnings of Qualified Manpower in England and Wales, 1966/67,* HMSO, 1971

SS4. As SS1, Part II: *The Curriculum.*

In addition there have been a number of reports sponsored by the Department on topics of particular concern. There have been four of particular educational importance, all containing some statistical material:

11. *The Crowther Report : 15 to 18,* a study made in 1956 by the Central Advisory Council for Education. The aim of this study was 'to find out more about 15- to 18-year-olds in education, work and leisure'.

Three separate investigations were made: one by the Government Social Survey, of 16 to 20-year-olds generally, one by the Army and RAF of their recruits aged 18 to 25 years, and one through Technical Colleges of 16- to 20-year-old students on technical courses.

This report provides a considerable amount of statistical information on topics which include:

Home background and other factors affecting the age of leaving school.
Education and employment since leaving school.
Leisure time activities.
Apprenticeships and other training.
Qualifications obtained at and after school.

12. *The Robbins Report : Higher Education,* a study made in the period 1961–63 by a Government Committee on Higher Education. Its terms of reference were 'to review the pattern of full-time education in Great Britain . . . and to advise on what principles its long-term development should be based'.

The report reviews changes over time in student numbers and courses taken and considers future demands. A large amount of statistical information is given, which includes:

School leavers qualified for further education.
Time series of students by age, sex, type of further education, qualifications before entry.
Staff qualifications and courses taken.
Financial and economic aspects.

13. *The Newsom Report: Half Our Future,* a study made in 1961–62 by the Central Advisory Council for Education. The aim of the study was 'to consider the education between the ages of 13 and 16 of pupils of average or less than average ability'.

This report differs from others in this section in providing little statistical data. Information tabulated includes:

Reading test scores by age, sex, area and type of school.
Time spent in different curriculum fields and subjects.

14. *The Plowden Report: Children and their Primary Schools,* a study made in the period 1963–66 by the Central Advisory Council for Education. The aim of the study was 'to consider the whole subject of primary education and the transition to secondary education'.

The second of the two volumes contains accounts of a number of surveys and research studies commissioned at the request of the Council. All concern some aspect of primary education and contain a variable amount of data. The most substantial are included in Appendices 3–6 where there is an analysis of the 1964 National Survey, an investigation conducted by the Government Social Survey into parental attitudes and circumstances related to school and pupil characteristics.

15. *Education Statistics for the U.K.* This annual volume was first published in 1967 and contains information extracted from the separate publications of the three education authorities of the UK. It is in three parts:

1. Outline of the UK educational system, under headings similar to those in volumes 1–6 of *Statistics of Education,* for the UK as a whole.

2. Sources: a valuable section providing a comprehensive review of current Department of Education and UGC publications, both regular and special.

3. Explanatory Notes on Tables: including notes on the assumptions made in the estimation of projected pupil numbers.

Publications of the University Grants Committee

16. *Returns from Universities and University Colleges in receipt of Exchequer Grants*. This annual report was discontinued in 1966 and the information it provided was incorporated into volume 6 of *Statistics of Education* (see 6).

17. *Annual Survey and Review of University Development*. This contains figures of student residence and places provided, and an account of expenditure on students, administration, etc.

18. *First Employment of University Graduates*. This is an annual publication, the first relating to graduates of the 1961–62 session from English and Welsh universities. The data are collected by the universities' Appointments Officers. Information concerning Scottish graduates has been published in Scottish Educational Statistics.

19. *Enquiry into Student Progress*. These enquiries are made 'from time to time' by the UGC 'in order to establish facts from which the extent of the problem [of student failure in degree courses] can be judged' as a basis for any necessary action.

Student entrants in 1950, 1952, 1955, 1957 and 1967 have been analysed, some early material being used in the Robbins Report (no. 12). The results of the 1952, 1955 and 1957 analyses were published in *University Development, 1957–62*. The 1967 report, published in 1968, was the first to name institutions and give results by subject groups.

Publications of the University Central Council for Admissions

20. The *Annual Report* gives figures of admissions, by sex, subject of first choice and subject of final acceptance, including those candidates applying through the clearing scheme.

21. *The Statistical Supplement* appears after the *Report* and gives a great deal more detail concerning candidates. This includes:

Parental occupation of accepted home candidates.
Proportion of candidates interviewed.

A survey of candidates unsuccessful in all applications, including
their destination.

1st degree achievements of earlier admissions.

'A' level grades of applicants.

*Publication of the Institute of Municipal Treasurers and Accountants
and the Society of County Treasurers*

22. *Education Statistics.* This annual publication provides statistics
at local education authority level. The information includes:

The number of pupils in each type of school, including nursery
schools, maintained and not maintained by a local education
authority.

The number of teachers and non-teaching staff in primary and
secondary schools.

The number of pupils over school leaving age.

Grants awarded.

The Census of Population

23. *Education Tables* (Table 9). Information on educational topics
collected in the postwar Censuses of Population has related to
terminal education age, current attendance at educational establishments and qualifications (Table 2). The first two are topics similar
to those of other publications in this section, that is, principally
relating to the institution and its structure. The 1951 Census
obtained information on this aspect alone, the data appearing in
the *General Tables,* one of the last Census volumes to be published,
where it was stated that it was not considered necessary to present
them in a separate report. The 1961 Census repeated the question
on terminal education age within the 10 per cent sample enquiry,
and results were this time among the first to be published in
an *Education* volume. This also contained tables associating
terminal education age with occupation and socio-economic
group—an aspect more closely related to the topics of the next
section.

THE INDIVIDUAL IN RELATION TO THE LABOUR FORCE

The Census of Population

24. *Qualification tables* (Table 9). The three Censuses of 1961, 1966 and 1971 all included questions concerned with qualifications, in increasing detail (Table 2). Scientific and Technological volumes have been published from 1961 (10 per cent sample) and 1966 Census data. An additional volume, *Qualified Manpower*—the first to give information on all types of qualification—was added in 1966 and involved new classifications of subject and qualifications (see p. 113).

The association of terminal education age with occupation in 1961 also belongs to this aspect of education.

Publications of the Department of Employment (and its predecessors). Few of this Department's statistics provide explicit information concerning qualifications in relation to employment—to date there are a relatively small number of occupational analyses published (Table 5*b*) and these cover a limited range of industries. However, the provision of such information has increased over recent years and the new series of industrial statistics will be useful in this respect. Two analyses are currently made which are relevant.

25. *Young persons entering employment.* Records from youth employment offices are used for an annual analysis of young persons under the age of 18 years entering employment for the first time. This is at a regional level and with a breakdown by age and sex. The employment entered is divided into five categories:

1. Apprenticeships.
2. Employment leading to professional qualifications.
3. Clerical employment.
4. Employment with other types of planned training.
5. Other.

Some omissions are indicated by the Department of Employment—for example, there is no account available of subsequent changes and therefore some apprenticeships taken up later are

TABLE 9
Education tables in postwar Censuses of Population

Subject	Census year	Level tabulated %	Related to:	Title of volume	Area (key, p. 111)
1. Terminal education age	1951	100	Sex	*General Tables*	2–6
			Age group		2–6
			Occupation (orders, selected units of occupational classification 1950)		2, 3
	1961	10	Sex	*Education Tables*	2–7
			Age group		2–4
			Occupation (orders, unit groups of occupational classification, 1960)		2
			Socio-economic group		2
2. Current attendance at an educational establishment	1951	100	Sex	*General Tables*	2–6
			Age group		2–6
3. Qualifications (see Table 2)	1961	10	Sex	*Scientific and Technological Qualifications*	1
			Age		1
			Occupation (orders, selected unit groups of occupational classification, 1960)		1
			Industry (orders, selected MLH groups of SIC 1958)		1
			Subject of qualification		1
			Country of birth		1
	1966	10	Sex	*Scientific and Technological Qualifications*	1
			Age		1
			Occupation group (defined in volume)		1
			Industry group (defined in volume)		1
			Country of birth		1
			Migration from abroad		1
			Postgraduate qualification		1
			Chartered engineers: 1st qualification		1

TABLE 9 *(cont'd)*

Subject	Census year	Level tabulated %	Related to :	Title of volume	Area (key below)
	1966	10	Sex	*Qualified*	1
			Age	*Manpower*	1
			Occupation (orders, and selected unit groups of occupational classification 1966)		1
			Industry (orders and selected MLH groups of SIC 1958)		1
			Economic activity		1
			Employment status		1
			Subject group*		1
			Level*		1
			Part-time, full-time		1
			Area of usual residence		1,2,3
	1971	10	No information available at the time of publication		

Key to areas
1. Great Britain
2. England and Wales
3. Region
4. Urban/Rural Aggregates
5. Conurbation
6. Local education authorities
7. Enumeration district.

* Special classifications defined in introduction to the volume (see text, pp. 113, 114).

excluded, and records of movement between educational establishments such as school to university are also not available. The age restriction of eighteen years is also a limiting factor.

26. *Local authority employees*. An annual analysis of the number of local authority employees, broken down by type of employment includes information on the number and distribution of lecturers and teachers employed by local authorities.

Publications of the Department of Education and Science and other Governmental Departments

A number of specialised publications concerned with qualifications and manpower have been introduced over recent years, and a comprehensive account of these is given by Whybrew.[2] They include:

27. *Statistics of Science and Technology 1967–70*. This annual publication was produced jointly by the Department of Education and Science and the Ministry of Technology between 1967 and 1970. It contains previously published material as well as new, from a variety of internal and external sources, concerning science and technology. It includes the following sections:

Data from surveys of scientific research and development including a financial breakdown between sectors providing and receiving funds.

Time series of first degree university graduates by sector of employment, subject of qualification and class of degree.

Time series of higher degree graduates by sector of employment and subject of qualification.

Time series of science graduates in education by age and type of school.

Students of science and technology in education.

Time series of GCE and CSE examination results in science subjects.

Reports of manpower surveys, 1962–65 and 1965–68.

Survey of professional engineers (1968 volume).

Survey of technicians (1967 volume).

28. *Studies in Technological Manpower.* These are publications by the Department of Trade and Industry. Relevant to this section to date is No. 3: *Persons with Qualifications in Engineering, Technology and Science, 1959–68,* published in 1971.

Classification schemes in the educational field are of recent development and are a further indication of an increasing acceptance of the need for quantitative information concerning, in particular, the reservoir of skill and its distribution within the country. Questions on qualifications in the two most recent Censuses of Population have provided data on a substantial scale which it was necessary to systematise in some way in order to use them to the maximum advantage.

Two classification schemes have therefore been evolved by the Department of Education and Science in consultation with other Government Departments and organisations with an interest in this problem, one a subject classification and the other a classification of qualifications. Both are described in the introduction to the *Qualified Manpower* volume of the 1966 Census in which they are used.

Subject classification

Eighty-six primary subjects are identified allocated to ten subject groups. The classification provides for the combination of two or more subjects.

Classification of qualifications

This classification applies to qualifications not normally obtained at school. Three levels are defined and all approved qualifications are listed within them in the *Qualified Manpower* volume.

Level *(a)*: higher university degrees.
Level *(b)*: first degrees and other qualifications of this or higher standard.

Level *(c)*: qualifications that generally satisfy three requirements: (1) they are obtained at the age of eighteen years or over; (2) they are above GCE 'A' level or CSE standard; (3) they are below first degree standard.

Sampling frames

Sampling frames are lists used to draw a random sample from a population, and should therefore theoretically contain every member of that population without duplication. Few sampling frames meet this requirement completely, but in the account which follows, those in most general use are described and the extent to which they deviate from the ideal is considered.

LISTS OF THE GENERAL POPULATION

1. *Register of Electors*

The Register of Electors is used as a sampling frame in the great majority of social surveys in this country. Although it has disadvantages as a frame—and it should be remembered that its publication is for election purposes rather than social survey—these are not so great as to invalidate its use, though they should be recognised. It may be purchased from the Registration Office in the town or county offices of the local authority concerned at a cost (currently) of 25p per 1000 names (reduced to 5p when it is sold to an election candidate).

Population listed. The Register is compiled annually from information obtained in a canvass held at the beginning of October. The local authority is responsible for employing canvassers to distribute forms to each household in their area on which the names of each member of the household, who is a British subject or a citizen of the Republic of Ireland, and who will have reached the age of eighteen within the period in which the register is in force—that is, one year from 16 February—must be given. Where the age of eighteen is only attained during this period, the date of birth must be stated. The forms are generally delivered by hand and a check is made at the time for any changes from the current register, but the 'occupier' is responsible for returning the form by post and this form is used to bring the current register up to date. Information given should relate to 10 October, although the registers come into force for election purposes from the following 16 February. The term 'occupier' used on the registration form is generally interpreted as the person responsible for payment of rates, and this person, whose name should appear first, will be liable for jury service except where his or her age is over sixty (in which case this must be stated) or the rateable value of the house falls below the qualifying amount (usually £20, except in the Greater London Area where it is £30). Joint house ownership is rarely taken into account and jury service tends therefore to fall in the great majority of cases to the male head of household. The names of lodgers must also be given and any other permanent residents. For example, people abroad on business or away in hospital should be included and if in the forces this should be indicated so that a postal vote can be allowed without query. Similarly in institutions such as hotels, hospitals or schools, the person in charge is responsible for providing the names of permanent residents. Temporary residents, of course, should be listed at their permanent address.

The Register of Electors therefore differs from the Census in asking for the names of permanent residents, whether they are temporarily absent at the time the forms are distributed, or not. Consequently the population contained in the register should approximate apart from age and nationality qualifications, to the 'Total' population or the Census population adjusted for usual residence place, plus British nationals abroad.

People with more than one address which they can consider their permanent residence, should generally register at the one they are in on 10 October. These are mainly persons working too far away from home to travel daily, most often living at one address from Monday to Friday and another over the weekend, and with students are by no means an insignificant proportion of the population. Since the 1969 Representation of the People Regulations, no name should appear more than once on the Register.

Form of listing. The integration of the information provided by electoral registration forms is the work of the local authorities' Electoral Registration Department, part of the Town or County Clerk's Department. Here the names on the forms are checked against those appearing by the same address on the previously compiled register. Where names have changed, those superseded are placed on a list which will become the 'C' register, while the new names are listed on what will be the 'B' register. On the main register, the new names are substituted for the old.

Except in those rural areas where all names are listed alphabetically whatever the address, members of the household are grouped together on the register with the occupier's name first. Others of the same surname headed if applicable by the wife follow with the rest usually in alphabetical order of Christian names. Households' members with different surnames appear next again usually in alphabetical order, though there is no requirement to do this. Within institutions again, residents may be listed in alphabetical order.

Only the permanent residents and staff of institutions and homes will be listed, for temporary residents should appear with other members of their household against their home address. This leads to one source of omissions either because such residents are not included by the person filling in the form at home, or if they are sole occupiers, because there is no one to see that their registration form is filled in for them.

Numbers or letters may appear against names in the register as follows:

(a) Two numbers separated by a dash: these denote the day and the month of birth, and indicate that the person against whose name they appear will reach the age of eighteen years on that date.

(b) J: denotes that the person is liable to be called for jury service, that is that they are responsible for the payment of rates, that the rateable value of their property reaches the qualifying amount of the area and usually that they are below the age of sixty years.

(c) M: denotes that the elector is a merchant seaman and therefore entitled to a postal vote if this is claimed.

(d) S: denotes a member of the armed forces, again entitled to a postal vote.

(e) L: denotes today only a peer of the realm, who is not entitled to vote at a parliamentary election. The appearance of non-residents with a property qualification on the register, entitled to vote at local elections, who used also to be identified by 'L', has been abolished since 1970.

Each Electoral Register usually lists the names and addresses of residents within a polling district, that is a district served by the same polling station at an election. At times, where a polling district is a large one, it will be split between two registers. A variable number of polling districts combine to form a constituency, and unlike most constituencies, the polling district boundaries coincide with the local authority boundary, following ward boundaries or otherwise combining within a ward. Most local authorities provide a street list which gives the number of the polling district in which each street or part street lies, and the polling district numbers corresponding to each ward. However, as the price of this list is statutorily fixed and does not often cover the cost of its production, only the larger authorities usually provide it.

Except in rural areas, the names and house numbers of electors are listed under street names arranged in alphabetical order, nowadays followed by their postal code. Each name is numbered consecutively on the left so that the total number of persons listed on the register will be the number attached to the last name on the register. On the right of each name is the number or name of the house or flat occupied. The names of large institutions usually head the list of their residents. It is not always easy to distinguish a small boarding house or hotel from a house divided into rooms or containing a number of lodgers. The type of institution may also not be immediately evident particularly where residents are of both sexes—many pensioner's homes, for example, are given names indistinguishable from a boarding house. If, as in many surveys, a sample is to be taken from only private households, it may be necessary to make a preliminary visit to check on the type of establishment listed.

In rural areas where the total number of residents and number of dwellings within each road tend to be few, names are often listed alphabetically without street headings. With such an arrangement, sampling by households is impossible without a preliminary sorting out.

Form of publication. The registers are first published in a provisional form at the end of November. They are then displayed in post offices and in the town or county hall so that residents may check that their names have been included. Omissions will chiefly be of those recently moved into the area. If a schedule has not been returned, but the household concerned appeared on the previous register, they are most likely to remain on the current register because it is not compiled each year anew, but by the amendment of the previous one.

In mid-December, the provisional registers are removed, revisions and corrections made and the final version is published in February. This is in force in the period between 16 February of the current year to 15 February of the following year.

As well as the main register, B and C registers can be bought, and may be of use in particular for surveys concerned with mobility. The B register contains the names of those appearing on the main register for the first time in the current year and therefore includes the following individuals:

(a) those who have moved into the area during the period covered by the previous register.

(b) those attaining the age of eighteen years during the period covered by the current register.

119

(c) those omitted in error from the previous register though resident for more than one year in the area—these will mainly be residents of one to two years standing.

The C register contains the names of those taken off the previous register and includes the following individuals:

(a) those who have moved out of the area during the period covered by the previous register.

(b) those who have died during the period covered by the previous register.

(c) those included in error on the previous register though not then resident in the area—mainly people who moved away one or two years previously.

Accuracy of the register. Assessments of the accuracy of the Electoral Register were made by the Government Social Survey in 1950[1] and 1966.[2]

Findings from the 1966 enquiry into the number of electors in private households appearing on the current register for their area were summarised as follows:

Proportion of eligible electors registered and still at the qualifying address (in private households)

On the qualifying date for registration (10 Oct. 1965)	When the Register came into force (16 Feb. 1966)	Halfway through the life of the Register (Aug. 1966)	At the end of the life of the Register (15 Feb. 1967)
96%	93%	89%	85%

At the time of this enquiry, unlike that of 1950, the names of young people reaching voting age during the life of the Register were preceded by a letter 'Y' (now replaced by date of birth). It was among this group that the greatest discrepancies were found, a total of 26 per cent not appearing on the Register at all.

Other groups found to be at risk in this respect were people who had recently moved—18 per cent of those with a different address a year previously were not listed, and members of a second family in the household, 15 per cent of whom were not registered. Others liable to be missed were the recently naturalised, boarders, domestic staff and tenants. Less than 1 per cent appeared on the Register twice. In spite of the omissions, Gray and Gee concluded that with the exception of the Y category, there had been a very slight improvement in registration since 1950.

Clearly, where a sample is to be selected from a rapidly growing area such as a new housing estate or New Town, it may well be that the number of occupied houses omitted is high, especially if selection is made during the summer or later. In this case, the registers must be supplemented from the lists held at the local Town or County Surveyor's Office. On completion of houses, builders are obliged to inform this office that they are ready for occupation and this information is recorded. The names of the expected occupiers are not included, and often full addresses are not provided, many houses being initially identified by plot numbers. However, the records may be used in the same way as the Electoral Register to provide a sample of addresses, and their location can usually be discovered. The main difficulty arises where they are situated on new unnamed roads.

Selection of a sample from the Register.[3] The Electoral Register is the most convenient sampling frame to use where a sample of households is required. In this case the address—that is the name or number of the dwelling with the street in which it is situated is used as the basic sampling unit.

Selection may be made in the following ways:

1. Addresses are numbered, care being taken to separate flats and rooms identified separately. For example, 15 and 15 (back), or 15 and 15A, must be counted separately. Selection is made by the use of random numbers or systematic sampling, after a random start.[4]

2. The number of addresses required in the sample is multiplied by 2.15[5] and a sampling fraction calculated as if for a sample of electors (see below). However, an address is selected *only if the appropriate number falls to the first person of the household.*

3. Use can be made of the consecutive numbers attached to each individual in the Register by first making a systematic selection of individuals who are placed on a list according to the total number of electors at the address. The sample is finally selected by taking each address where only one elector has been listed, alternate addresses where two have been listed, and so on. The result is a sample in which each household has an equal probability of selection.[6]

Where, on interviewing, it is found that more than one household occupies the dwelling selected, an adjustment must be made to keep the proportion of multi-occupying households sampled comparable to that in the population. The method which retains the correct proportionate distribution of households by size has been described by Gray and Corlett:

All the households in the dwelling are included in the sample and succeeding addresses are omitted equivalent to the additional households included, e.g. if two households are present, the next address is omitted: if three, the next two are omitted. Multi-occupancy can lead to difficulties of contact, and a ruling is usually made that a maximum of three households at one address are interviewed.[7]

Clearly the Register can only be used without modification as a sampling frame of individuals of either or both sexes, where those eighteen years old or over are of interest, or where other sources are available for the younger age groups. Where selected age groups, or individuals below the age of eighteen years unobtainable from other sources, or other specially composed groups are required, the Register can be used to select households whose composition is then obtained on interview when the required individuals can be identified. In this case, allowance must be made in the size of the sample for those households without members of the type required, and an estimate of the proportions involved can usually be obtained from Census data. Care must be taken where more than one individual of the group required is found in one household and selection may then be made by the interviewer according to a predetermined scheme. An alternative is for a second frame to be constructed containing only those of the required group after interviewing all households in the area, but this method is only practicable where the population is a small one.

To draw a sample of electors, a simple random or systematic sample may be taken, the latter after a random start, and as each individual is already numbered in the registers, this type of selection is a simple matter. Where more than one register is involved, the first number of each succeeding register must be added to the last number of the previous one to provide a consecutive series. A computer programme may be devised from which random numbers are generated using the total number of individuals or addresses involved. These may be sorted into order within each register, and distributed in their original form.[8]

2. *Rating lists*

Rating lists, like the Register of Electors also provide lists of addresses contained within a local authority area. The name of the householder is also given, but no information on the number of occupants. Unlike the Register of Electors, rating lists include all types of property, whether residential or not, with a description of their use. They also state the rateable value of the property—one of the advantages of rating lists, in indicating, though roughly, the approximate income group and status of the occupier. However, the rateable values of properties become less and less reliable guides to the circumstances of their owners, and are rarely used nowadays in this way.

The main advantage given by rating lists compared with the Register of Electors, is that they are likely to be more complete, for the inclusion of a property on the list does not depend on a return from the householder. New houses are entered on the list for rating purposes when occupied and remain there until demolition. The names of new occupiers are substituted when the property changes hands. However, the 1966 sample Census demonstrated that there may be a greater time lag between occupation and entry than was realised. The use of rating lists to up-date 1961 Census records of residential property led to substantial under enumeration (see p. 27).

INTERNAL MIGRANTS

No sampling frame available lists all internal migrants, but a number of incomplete sources exist. Some of these were examined by the North Regional Planning Committee's research team in 1966 as a preliminary to their survey of mobility.[9] Much of the following information is summarised from this report.

Out-migrants

Identification of persons who have moved out of an area is difficult, but possible sources are:

Removal contractor's records. These records could provide the addresses of the majority of families moving out of an area, but it was found by the N.R.P.C. that about half the contractors they contacted were unwilling to disclose this information—a difficulty almost certain to be met elsewhere.

National Health Service Executive Council records. These records relate to changes of doctor and would therefore omit those people moving short distances and not making such a change. Other deficiencies in medical records are considered in detail below in relation to doctors' records. Confidentiality is again a factor here as well as the difficulty involved in extracting the information.

Gas Board records. Incomplete coverage is a drawback here, as well as the form in which the records are kept.

Electricity Board records. The availability of these records depends on the policy of the particular Board concerned, and the form taken by its final accounts. If available, they would appear to be the best source of out-migrants' addresses, though again one which is by no means complete. Persons moving out of rooms or other lodgings whose rent has included electricity or who use a meter, will form the greater part of the omissions. Such people will mainly be in younger age groups, single and living away from their parents—typically a highly mobile group.

In-migrants
The B Register. The majority of migrants moving into an area may be identified by using the B register of the Register of Electors, already described.

In order to identify migrants, as opposed to those appearing on this register because they have reached the appropriate age, surnames must be compared with those at the same address, appearing in the main register. In the great majority of cases, the same surname denotes a newly qualified voter in the family, while nearly all other cases are those who have moved into the polling district since the previous register was compiled.

The reliability of the B register in identifying migrants was assessed by the North Regional Planning Committee, who compared the number of migrants extracted from the list with those discovered in a complete census of a number of areas. It was estimated from the analysis of results that in the North Region generally, about 15 per cent of in-migrants would not be picked up from this register. The proportion varies from area to area, rising to 29 per cent in areas with high multi-occupation. Such areas typically contain a very mobile population, who may depend on landlords for their inclusion on the annual registration form.

Records held by the local education authority. These records give the change of address of children moving into and out of the authority (see below). They would appear to be a useful source of information concerning families containing children of school age, though will omit children attending special, public or private schools—in many areas a negligible total.

OTHER SPECIAL GROUPS

Where a sample is required of a group which occurs widely among the population—for example, manual workers, economically active men, or families containing both parents and children—the Register of Electors or Rating Lists may still be the best frames available. Preferably, an area is chosen in which there is known to be a higher than average proportion of the group to be studied. Census data will normally provide this information for most group characteristics likely to be of interest and also provide an estimate of the proportion of the population taken by the group. The accuracy of this estimate will depend on the length of time which has elapsed since the previous Census and the stability of the area. The size of sample for analysis is then increased to allow for those individuals or households appearing in the selected sample who do not belong to the required group. The interviewer usually determines, in the initial stages of the interview, whether the respondent falls into this category and if not the interview is terminated. An alternative method is to construct a sampling frame by initial enquiry and use this to select the final sample.

Both methods can be laborious and expensive, specially if the group which is of interest is a relatively small one, and in this case it is usually more practical to make use of any lists which are more specific, even though they are likely to be less accurate. Most market research organisations will make initial enquiries in an area and provide lists, though this is an additional expense, and the reliability of the lists is an unknown factor—clearly the more thorough the enquiry, the more expensive. Government offices often have suitable information, but are rarely willing to disclose it, however much they approve of the use to which it might be put, for they consider the importance of confidentiality to be paramount. Other authorities may be more flexible if the expected results are seen to be worthwhile though will still expect the confidentiality of any information provided to be safeguarded. Some lists which may be made available are discussed in the following sections.

School records

Records of present and past pupils at schools administered by the local education authority are held at the school and by the authority. The latter are believed by the North Regional

Planning Committee to be 'fairly comprehensive' as far as children attending school within the authority are concerned, and give the change of address of children, both moving in and out of the authority.

Within the school, records include the address during attendance at the school. The length of time for which the records of past pupils are kept varies, and addresses soon become unreliable. Other information normally collected includes the occupation of the parent, the number of brothers and sisters and, of course, date of birth, previous schools, if any, results of any IQ or similar tests.

The catchment areas of schools are variable and usually overlap with adjacent schools. Children attending public, private and special schools must be borne in mind, if all children in an area are of interest. Where parents have choice, for example of secondary grammar schools, there will be a tendency for them to select schools according to known characteristics which appeal to them, e.g. a high academic standard, or an interest in games. Pupils are therefore in such cases never a random selection of children living in the neighbourhood.

Pay-rolls

Most firms and companies maintain lists of their employees which include their address, age and qualifications as well as occupation in the firm and pay. Records concerning previous employees vary considerably and as a move from a firm is often associated with a change of address, a biased sample will result when use is made of such information as the more mobile who tend to be lost differ in many characteristics from the more stable. Reasons for leaving the firm may be recorded but these tend to be of dubious value.

Doctor's records

Records of patients kept by their general practitioner have been used on a number of occasions to obtain lists of individuals with characteristics occurring in a small proportion of the general population. Retirement pensioners are a well-known example.

Doctors' records include the patients' address, date of birth, sex and marital status as well as his medical history.

Evidence suggests that these records are less reliable than has often been appreciated by those who have used them. Apart from their reliability they have two initial disadvantages:

1. The area covered by a GP's practice does not correspond to any administrative area. It extends to a variable distance from his surgery within his Local Executive Council Area—a distance of his own choosing and dependent on factors which vary from one doctor to another.

2. A GP's patients are not a random selection of residents in his area. GPs tend to attract certain groups—for example, some gain a reputation for being 'good with children', others as attentive to the elderly, and others as unwilling to provide sickness notes. Socio-economic and age groups therefore frequently occur in proportions very different from those of the population in the catchment area. If these lists are to be used to select what is hoped to be a random sample of certain sections of the general population, then for this reason, lists from as many practices as possible in the locality should be used.

Other discrepancies also occur in these lists. Although it was estimated that a high proportion of the population is registered with a doctor, the omissions are almost certainly a highly selected group especially in terms of age. In addition a time lag is usual between moving to an area and registration with a doctor, which will be particularly lengthy in the case of those least likely to need a doctor's services, such as those in the age group fifteen to twenty-five years of age, who are a particularly mobile group.

A timelag also occurs between a death and the removal of the record from the list, a factor needing to be taken into account especially in retirement towns. Rees[10] has estimated that patient registrations exceed the number of *bona fide* patients by about 4·1 per cent, largely because of such records, and has found that inflation is higher in urban than rural areas, and highest in Greater London, Kent and Surrey. On the other hand, under-registration occurs in the Northern Region and East Anglia. There are a number of reasons why registration with a GP may not occur:

1. Persons treated by the medical services of the UK armed forces.
2. Persons treated by the medical services of Commonwealth and foreign armed forces.
3. Long-stay hospital patients.
4. Persons treated by prison medical services or other institutional services.
5. Persons receiving private medical attention exclusively.
6. A recent entrant to the UK, not yet registered.
7. Persons previously registered with an NHS doctor whom they no longer regard as theirs. These are mainly people who have moved recently, people whose doctor has retired or died and people obtaining medical treatment from other parts of the NHS.

In a survey of people aged eighty years or over made by Frazer Brockington,[11] GPs' lists were used to identify residents of this age group in Stockport, as well as other sources, such as health visitors' lists, advertisements in doctors' surgeries, appeals on the radio and in the Press, in-patients records and enquiries by social workers. Using death registrations to give the proportion of this age group in the population it was estimated that 23 per cent had been missed, the greatest discrepancy occurring among those at the lower end of the group. This confirms that GPs' lists are less comprehensive than is generally appreciated and their limitations as sampling frames should be recognised, though this does not mean that they may not be the best available source for locating minority groups.

Youth Club membership lists
Use has been made of youth clubs to obtain samples of adolescents. Such a sample will be unrepresentative of this age group, for membership of these clubs is a minority activity, even when an adequate number to serve the total population is available. For example, in Kirkby in 1964 where clubs were run by the schools,

churches and other organisations it was estimated that three-quarters of young people between fourteen and twenty years old were unattached to any organised group.[12] Duplication will also occur within the lists of clubs for those who join frequently join more than once.

Educational establishments

A number of publications provide lists of educational establishments. The most comprehensive is the Education Committee's *Year Book* which lists, within the UK,

(a) All schools except primary schools, by counties.

(b) Universities, Polytechnics and Colleges of Education by counties.

(c) Other Colleges, e.g. Agricultural, Arts and Crafts, Physical Education, Adult Education.

(d) Firms providing facilities for student apprentices.

(e) Special Schools, approved schools.

A similarly comprehensive book which also gives the number of pupils in the schools, and again includes all except primary schools, is the Education Authorities *Directory* published by the School Government Publishing Co. This also gives a separate alphabetical list (under authorities) of Youth Employment Service Offices, libraries and 'organisations concerned with education', such as Community Volunteers Organisation, the Outward Bound Trust, the English Folk Dance and Song Society, etc.

There are a number of publications listing public, independent and preparatory schools. These include:

The Public and Preparatory School Yearbook ed. J. F. Burnel, A. & C. Black

The Girls' School Year Book, A. & C. Black (public and preparatory schools)

The Schools of England, Wales, Scotland and Ireland, ed. J. Burrow (girls' and boys' public and independent schools)

Businesses

A Directory of Businesses is to be published as parts 159–171 of the *Census of Production 1968*. This is a list of respondents to the Census who have agreed voluntarily to allow the publication of their names and addresses. It was stated by the Board of Trade that the 'majority' agreed, but without giving any other indication of the proportion covered.

Businesses providing information for this Census are those industries included in Orders II to XXI of the Standard Industrial Classification.

A Central Register of Businesses is at present being compiled by the Business Statistics Office of the Central Statistical Office, one of its functions being 'to provide a frame for the choosing of samples'.[13] How far this register will be made available to *bona fide* users is conjectural but it could be invaluable to research workers in the industrial field. Establishments will be listed by area, size and type, classified at the minimum list heading level of the 'Standard Industrial Classification'.

Employers associations, trade unions, etc.

A list of these associations was published by the Ministry of Labour in 1960 and is kept up to date by amendments every few months. The original volume, *Directory of Employers Associations, Trade Unions, Joint Organisations, etc.*, includes also the names of Standing Joint Industrial Councils, Conciliation and Arbitration Boards and other similar bodies.

Appendix

Standard Regions and conurbations

The Standard Regions and their Constituent Authorities, 1950–72.
England and Wales 1950–65

REGION I
Northern

Cumberland
Durham
Northumberland
Westmorland
Yorkshire, North
  Riding

REGION II
*East and
West Ridings*
Yorkshire, East
  Riding
Yorkshire, West
  Riding

REGION III
North Midland
Derbyshire, Part of[1]
Leicestershire
Lincolnshire:
  Parts of Holland
  Parts of Kesteven
  Parts of Lindsey
Northamptonshire
Nottinghamshire
Peterborough,
  Soke of
Rutland

REGION IV
Eastern

Bedfordshire
Cambridgeshire
Ely, Isle of
Essex, Part of[2]
Hertfordshire,
  Part of[3]
Huntingdonshire
Norfolk
Suffolk, East
Suffolk, West

REGION V
*London and South
Eastern*
Essex, Part of[4]
Hertfordshire,
  Part of[5]
Kent
London Admin.
  County
Middlesex
Surrey
Sussex, East
Sussex, West

REGION VI
Southern

Berkshire
Buckinghamshire
Dorset, Part of[6]
Hampshire
Oxfordshire
Wight, Isle of

REGION VII
South Western
Cornwall
Devon
Dorset, Part of[7]
Gloucestershire
Somerset
Wiltshire

REGION VIII
*Wales I
(South East)*
Brecknockshire
Carmarthenshire
Glamorganshire
Monmouthshire

WALES II
(remainder)
Anglesey
Caernarvonshire
Cardiganshire
Denbighshire
Flintshire
Merionethshire
Montgomeryshire
Pembrokeshire

Radnorshire

REGION IX
Midlands
Herefordshire
Shropshire
Staffordshire
Warwickshire
Worcestershire

REGION X
North Western
Cheshire
Derbyshire, Part of[8]
Lancashire

---

1. All except Buxton MB, Glossop MB, New Mills UD, Whaley Bridge UD, and Chapel-en-le-Frith RD.
2. All except East Ham CB, West Ham CB, Chingford MB, Wanstead and Woodford MB, Leyton MB, Walthamstow MB, Ilford MB, Barking MB, Dagenham MB, Waltham Holy Cross UD and Chigwell UD.
3. All except Barnet UD, Bushey UD, Cheshunt UD, East Barnet UD, and Elstree RD.
4. All areas stated in 2 above.
5. All areas stated in 3 above.
6. Poole MB only.
7. All areas except Poole MB.
8. All areas stated in 1 above.

England and Wales 1965–72

North
Cumberland
Durham
Northumberland
Westmorland
Yorkshire, North Riding

Yorkshire and Humberside
Lincolnshire, Parts of
  Lindsey
Yorkshire, East Riding
Yorkshire, West Riding

North West
Cheshire
Derbyshire (part)[1]
Lancashire

East Midlands
Derbyshire (part)[2]
Leicestershire
Lincolnshire, Parts
  of Holland
Lincolnshire, Parts
  of Kesteven
Northamptonshire
Nottinghamshire
Rutland

West Midlands
Herefordshire
Shropshire
Staffordshire
Warwickshire
Worcestershire

East Anglia
Cambridgeshire and
  Isle of Ely
Huntingdon and
  Peterborough
Norfolk
Suffolk, East
Suffolk, West

South East
Bedfordshire
Berkshire
Buckinghamshire
Dorset (part)[3]
Essex
Greater London
Hampshire
Hertfordshire
Kent
Oxfordshire
Surrey
Sussex, East
Sussex, West
Wight, Isle of

South West
Cornwall
Devon
Dorset (part)[4]
Gloucestershire
Somerset
Wiltshire

Wales I (South East)
Breconshire
Carmarthenshire
Glamorgan
Monmouthshire

Wales II (remainder)
Anglesey
Caernarvonshire
Cardiganshire
Denbighshire
Flintshire
Merionethshire
Montgomeryshire
Pembrokeshire
Radnorshire

Notes:
1. Buxton MB, Glossop MB, New Mills UD, Whaley Bridge UD and Chapel-en-le-Frith RD.
2. All except areas stated in 1 above.
3. Poole MB only.
4. All except Poole MB.

Scotland

The regional divisions adopted for the purposes of the 1966 census are defined as follows:

West Central
Glasgow County of City
Ayr County
Bute County
Dunbarton County
Lanark County
Renfrew County

East Central
Edinburgh County of City
Clackmannan County
East Lothian County
Fife County
Kinross County
Midlothian County
Stirling County
West Lothian County

North Eastern
Aberdeen County of City
Dundee County of City
Aberdeen County
Angus County
Banff County
Kincardine County
Moray County
Nairn County
Perth County

Crofting Counties
Argyll County
Caithness County
Inverness County
Orkney County
Ross and Cromarty County
Sutherland County
Zetland County

South Western
Dumfries County
Kirkcudbright County
Wigtown County

Border Counties
Berwick County
Peebles County
Roxburgh County
Selkirk County

CONURBATIONS

The conurbation areas each consist of an aggregation of entire local authority areas and are constituted as follows:

Tyneside

Durham (part)

Gateshead CB
South Shields CB

Felling UD
Hebburn UD
Jarrow MB
Whickham UD

Northumberland (part)

Newcastle upon
  Tyne CB
Tynemouth CB
Gosforth UD
Longbenton UD
Newburn UD

Wallsend MB
Whitley Bay MB

West Yorkshire

Yorkshire, West Riding (part)

Bradford CB
Dewsbury CB
Halifax CB
Huddersfield CB
Leeds CB
Wakefield CB

Aireborough UD
Baildon UD
Batley MB
Bingley UD
Brighouse MB

Colne Valley UD
Denby Dale UD
Denholme UD
Elland UD
Heckmondwike UD
Holmfirth UD

Horbury UD
Horsforth UD
Keighley MB
Kirkburton UD
Meltham UD

Mirfield UD
Morley MB
Ossett MB
Pudsey MB
Queensbury and
  Shelf UD
Ripponden UD
Rothwell UD
Shipley UD
Sowerby Bridge UD
Spenborough MB
Stanley UD

South East Lancashire

Cheshire (part)

Stockport CB

Alderley Edge UD
Altrincham MB
Bowdon UD
Bredbury and
  Romiley UD
Cheadle and Gatley UD

Dukinfield MB

Lancashire (part)

Bolton CB
Bury CB
Manchester CB
Oldham CB
Rochdale CB
Salford CB

Ashton-under-Lyne
  MB
Audenshaw UD

Kearsley UD
Lees UD
Littleborough UD
Little Lever UD
Middleton MB
Milnrow UD
Mossley MB
Prestwich MB
Radcliffe MB
Royton UD

CONURBATIONS *(cont'd)*

South East Lancashire *(Cont.)*

Cheshire (part)

Hale UD
Hazel Grove and
    Bramhall UD
Hyde MB

Marple UD
Sale MB
Stalybridge MB
Wilmslow UD
Disley RD

Lancashire (part)

Chadderton UD
Crompton UD
Denton UD

Droylsden UD
Eccles MB
Failsworth UD
Farnworth MB
Heywood MB
Horwich UD
Irlam UD

Stretford MB
Swinton and
    Pendlebury MB
Tottington UD
Urmston UD
Wardle UD

Westhoughton UD
Whitefield UD
Whitworth UD
Worsley UD

Merseyside

Cheshire (part)

Birkenhead CB
Wallasey CB

Bebington MB

Ellesmere Port MB
Hoylake UD
Neston UD
Wirral UD

Lancashire (part)

Bootle CB
Liverpool CB

Crosby MB
Huyton-with-Roby
    UD
Litherland UD

West Midlands *(before 1 April 1966)*

Staffordshire (part)

Smethwick CB
Walsall CB
West Bromwich CB
Wolverhampton CB

Aldridge UD
Amblecote UD
Bilston MB
Brierley Hill UD
Coseley UD

Darlaston UD
Rowley Regis MB
Sedgley UD
Tettenhall UD
Tipton MB

Wednesbury MB
Wednesfield UD
Willenhall UD

Warwickshire (part)

Birmingham CB
Solihull CB

Sutton Coldfield MB

Worcestershire (part)

Dudley CB

Halesowen MB
Oldbury MB
Stourbridge MB

CONURBATIONS *(cont'd)*

West Midlands (from 1 April 1966)

Staffordshire (part)	Warwickshire (part)	Worcestershire (part)
Dudley CB	Birmingham CB	Warley CB
Walsall CB	Solihull CB	
West Bromwich CB		Halesowen MB
Wolverhampton CB	Sutton Coldfield MB	Stourbridge MB
Aldridge-Brownhills UD		

Greater London

Greater London Council Area

Clydeside

Glasgow County of City
In Dunbarton County
Clydebank Large Burgh
Bearsden Small Burgh
Kirkintilloch Small Burgh
Milngavie Small Burgh

In Lanark County
Airdrie Large Burgh
Coatbridge Large Burgh
Hamilton Large Burgh
Motherwell and Wishaw
   Large Burgh
Rutherglen Large Burgh
Bishopbriggs Small Burgh
East Kilbride Small Burgh
No. 6 District of County
No. 8 District of County
No. 9 District of County

In Renfrew County
Paisley Large Burgh
Barrhead Small Burgh
Johnstone Small Burgh
Renfrew Small Burgh
First District of County
Second District of County

References, notes,
and secondary sources

CHAPTER I. POPULATION AND THE CENSUS

1. The Registrar General's *Statistical Review,* part iii, *Commentary,* 1967, p. 4.

2. P. Geddes, *Cities in Evolution,* 1915.

3. *Statistical Review,* part ii, p. vii.

4. Census 1951, *Report on Greater London and Five other Conurbations,* p. xviii.

5. From the Explanatory Notes in 1961 county reports.

6. In 1970 the General Register Office (GRO) for England and Wales and the Government Social Survey merged into the Office of Population Censuses and Surveys. The office responsible for the Census of Population will therefore be termed GRO where pre-1970 activities are referred to, and after that period, OPCS.

7. Oxford Census Tract Committee, *Census 1951, Oxford area,* Oxford 1957.

8. The attempt to use 1961 boundaries in 1966 is described on p. 11.

9. P. Gray and F. Gee, 'The 1966 ten per cent Sample Census. Why there was no Preliminary Report', *Statistical News,* no. 10, 1970, p. 10, HMSO.

10. Census 1951, *General Report,* HMSO 1958, p. 11.

11. F. P. Boston and A. A. Cusion, '1971 Population Census', *Statistical News,* no. 12, 1971, p. 13.

12. The Registrar General's *Statistical Review 1966,* part iii, *Commentary,* 1969.

13. Census 1961, *Migration Tables,* HMSO, 1966, p. vii.

14. An account of this Survey is given in the Registrar General's *Statistical Review for 1966,* part iii, *Commentary.*

15. 1951 Census, *General Report,* p. 32.

16. 1961 Census, *General Report,* HMSO, 1968, p. 52.

17. *Ibid.,* pp. 45–54 contain a description of methods used.

18. *Ibid.,* pp. 50, 51.

19. These revisions are given for five-year age groups in the *Statistical Review for 1967,* part iii, *Commentary.*

20. *Ibid.,* p. 2.

CHAPTER 2.   OTHER CENSUS TOPICS

1. B. Benjamin, *The Population Census,* Heinemann for SSRC, 1970.

2. Census 1961, *General Report,* HMSO, 1968, p. 181.

3. See ch. 1, note 6.

4. Census 1951, *General Report,* 1958, pp. 36–56.

5. *Ibid.,* p. 57.

6. *The Registrar General's Quarterly Return for England and Wales,* quarter ended June 1971, HMSO, 1972.

7. See E. Gittus, Appendix A in C. Vereker, J. B. Mays *et al., Urban Redevelopment and Social Change*: Liverpool University Press, 1961.

8. Census 1961, *General Report,* p. 96.

9. 1971 Census, *Information Paper* no. 4.

10. Census 1951, *General Report,* p. 68.

11. H. Silcock, 'Sampling and the Census', *The Town Planning Review,* vol. 23, no. 4, January 1953, p. 316.

12. *Ibid.,* p. 317.

13. Census 1951, *General Report,* p. 7.

14. 49,300 in 1951; 68,900 in 1961; 102,000 in 1971.

CHAPTER 3.   THE LABOUR FORCE

1. *Report on the Census of Distribution and Other Services,* 1966, HMSO, 1970, pp. 1–8.

2. Minimum list headings 820 and 821 in the revised Standard Industrial Classification of 1968 and services.

3. *Census of Production Reports,* HMSO, *Guides to Official Sources,* no. 6, 1961.

4. Orders II to XXI as defined by the revised Standard Industrial Classification of 1968.

5. An account of the new series of enquiries is given by J. Stafford, 'The development of industrial statistics', *Statistical News,* no. 1, May 1968.

6. Interdepartmental Committee on Social and Economic Research, *Labour Statistics,* HMSO, *Guides to Official Sources,* no. 1, 1958.

7. Department of Employment, *British Labour Statistics Historical Abstract, 1886–1968,* HMSO, 1971.

8. E. Devons, *An Introduction to British Economic Statistics,* Cambridge University Press, 1958.

9. See 'Regional employment statistics', *Ministry of Labour Gazette,* vol. 74, July 1966, p. 389.

10. The publication of *Housing Statistics* and the *Monthly Bulletin of Construction Statistics* ends in 1972 and is replaced by *Housing and Construction Statistics* which includes information from both periodicals.

11. *Ministry of Labour Gazette,* November 1965, p. 480.

12. For definitions, see p. 71.

13. *Employment and Productivity Gazette,* vol. 78, Sept. 1970, pp. 780–4.

14. 'Differences between Standard Regions for statistical purposes and Ministry of Labour Administrative Regions', *Ministry of Labour Gazette,* vol. 74, 1966, p. 70.

15. *Ministry of Labour Gazette,* vol. 73, November 1965, p. 480.

16. *Classification of Occupations, 1960,* HMSO, 1960, p. vi.

17. *Classification of Occupations, 1970,* HMSO, 1970, p. vi.

18. S. Tolson, 'New occupational classification', *Dept. of Employment Gazette,* Jan. 1972, p. 3.

19. *Classification of Occupations, 1970,* p. x.

20. *Classification of Occupations, 1960,* p. xi.

21. See R. E. Beales, 'Standard industrial classification, 1968', *Statistical News,* no. 3, 1968.

22. *Ministry of Labour Gazette,* 1960, pp. 97–9.

23. *Employment and Productivity Gazette,* 1970, pp. 288–93.

CHAPTER 4.   EDUCATION

1. Central Advisory Council for Education, *15 to 18,* HMSO, 1956 (the Crowther Report).

2. E. G. Whybrew, 'Qualified manpower: statistical series', *Statistical News,* no. 17, May 1972.

REFERENCES, NOTES AND SECONDARY SOURCES

CHAPTER 5.   SAMPLING FRAMES

1. P. G. Gray, Corlett and Frankland, *The Register of Electors as a Sampling Frame,* Govt. Social Survey, 1950.

2. P. G. Gray and F. A. Gee, *Electoral Registration for Parliamentary Elections,* Govt. Social Survey, 1967.

3. A detailed account of the use of the Register to draw samples for either interview or postal surveys is given by S. Gray in *The Electoral Register,* Government Social Survey M. 151, 1971.

4. See C. A. Moser, *Survey Methods in Social Investigation,* Heinemann, 1958, pp. 76, 77; Moser uses the term 'quasi-random' rather than 'systematic'.

5. The average number of electors per address: see S. Gray, *op. cit.*

6. Moser, p. 125.

7. See P. G. Gray and T. Corlett, 'Sampling for the Social Survey', *Journal of the Royal Statistical Society,* Series A. vol. 113, part 2, 1950, p. 25.

8. A programme for selecting a simple random sample from a series of registers is available from the author at a small charge to cover printing, cost and postage.

9. *Mobility in the North,* vol. 3, *Research Techniques,* North Regional Planning Committee, 1967.

10. M. S. Rees, 'The inflation of N.H.S. registers of patients and its effect on the renumeration of GPs', *J. Roy. Stat. Soc.* vol. 132, part 4, 1969, p. 526.

11. Frazer Brockington and S. Lampert, *The Social Needs of the Over 80s,* Manchester University Press, 1966.

12. Estimate made by the Divisional Education Officer, see K. Pickett and D. Boulton, *Migration and Social Adjustment,* Liverpool University Press, 1973.

13. L. S. Berman, 'The Central Register of Businesses', *Statistical News,* no. 4, Feb. 1969.

The following publications are published currently on a regular rather than occasional basis. Those which include statistics bring together data from a number of sources, usually as a time series.

STATISTICS OF POPULATION, LABOUR, EDUCATION AND OTHER TOPICS

(a) National coverage

1. Central Statistical Office, *Annual Abstract of Statistics*. The statistics published are derived from Government departments and are in the form of annual statistics mainly in a nine-year series. Sources are given for each table and there is also an Index of Sources tabulated by subject, the Government Department responsible, and the publication or source in which they are first available.

Area: UK, Great Britain, and countries within the UK.

2. Central Statistical Office, *Monthly Digest of Statistics*. The statistics published are derived from Government departments and generally cover a period of six to seven years. The most recent monthly totals or averages are given where available, and some quarterly figures.

Area: UK, Great Britain, and countries within the UK.

3. Central Statistical Office, *Abstract of Regional Statistics* (annual). The statistics published are those analysed at regional level and where possible by subdivisions of regions in England and Wales, derived from Government Departments.

(b) Below national coverage

In these publications the statistics basically relate to single authorities although there may be comparative figures for Great Britain or England and Wales and are derived from central and local Government Departments.

1. Scottish Development Department (Economic and Statistics Unit), *Scottish Abstract of Statistics* (annual). This replaced the Digest of Scottish Statistics, enlarging some sections and giving additional information on sources.

2. Welsh Office, *Digest of Welsh Statistics* (annual).

3. Economic Section of the Cabinet Office, Belfast, *Digest of Statistics, Northern Ireland* (twice a year).

4. G.L.C. Research and Intelligence Unit, *Annual Abstract of Greater London Statistics*.

5. City of Birmingham Central Statistical Office, *City of Birmingham Abstract of Statistics* (annual).

6. Research and Intelligence Unit, Cheshire County Council, *Abstract of Statistics for the County of Cheshire*. The first publication, in 1972, covered the period 1970–71.

LABOUR STATISTICS

Department of Employment, *Year book of Labour Statistics 1969* (etc.). First published in 1971 when 1969 statistics were included, this is to be an annual publication and has replaced *Statistics of Incomes, Prices, Employment and Production*. It brings together the main series of statistics published in the *Department of Employment Gazette* during the year. Comparable Statistics for years previous to 1969 have been published in *British Labour Statistics Historical Abstract, 1886–1968*. Both volumes contain Introductory Notes which describe the methods by which the figures have been obtained.

SOURCE LIST

1. A useful index of current Government statistical sources (it does not contain statistics) is the Central Statistical Office, *List of Principal Statistical Series and Publications, 1972*. Amendments and additions are to be summarised in Statistical News.

2. The *Index* attached to the *Annual Abstract of Statistics* is described above.

NOTES ON SOURCES

An *Annual Supplement* to the *Monthly Digest of Statistics* gives definitions and explanatory notes which equally apply to the *Annual Abstract* and *Abstract of Regional Statistics*.

Index